POSITIVIST

ARTICLES, REVIEWS,

and LETTERS.

REPRINTED FROM THE BENGALEE.

[REVISED.]

CALCUTTA:

PRINTED AND PUBLISHED BY ANNADA PRASAD CHATTERJEE AT THE
BENGALEE PRESS, 336, CHITPORE ROAD.

1870.

CONTENTS.

PAGE.

I.—MISCELLANEOUS ARTICLES.

1.—The importance of Positivism, and the preparation necessary for the study of it 1
2.—The Abstract Sciences form a natural scale 5
3.—Social aim of Positivism 7
4.—On Caste 9
5.—Father Hyacinthe 14
6.—On Utilitarianism 18

II.—REVIEWS.

1.—Rationalism and Faith 26
2.—The Fortnightly on Utilitarianism 32
3.—The Religious Tendencies of India 50
4.—Dr. Sircar on Scientific Education 66
5.—The Contemporary Review on Positivism 74

III.—LETTERS.

1.—Positivism and Atheism 84
2.—The Aim of Positivism 86
3.— { (a) Positivism not Deism
      (b) Hindoo Theologism 89
4.—On Miracles 91
5.—Rev. K. S. Macdonald on Comte 93
6.—On Divorce 96
7.—Rev. Dr. M. Mitchell on Comte 100
8.—Property and its Duties 104

PREFACE.

THE contents of this pamphlet are for the most part the same as when they appeared in the columns of the *Bengalee*. Some of the articles, however, have been revised, and considerable additions have been made to a few of the letters.

The last of the Reviews, it will be observed, is almost wholly extracted from the *Contemporary*. It may perhaps be thought scarcely justifiable to quote so largely in an article which is styled a Review. The practice is certainly unusual, but some excuse may be afforded by the consideration that this pamphlet will circulate chiefly among readers who are not likely to be able to procure the original. As Positivism is too often regarded merely as an ingenious Philosophy, built upon science, it seemed desirable to furnish a concise yet accurate view of its religious system. For this purpose the Rev. B. F. Westcott's paper appeared to be admirably adapted; both on account of its intrinsic merits, and as exhibiting the influence exercised by Positivism on the mind of a sincere and accomplished theologian.

In every question that has been discussed, it will be seen that the same point of view has been uniformly adopted. The very fact that Positivism is thus able, on all occasions, to furnish the inquirer with a consistent and intelligible theory, affords the surest guarantee of its ultimate success. It was said by them of old, *Quot homines, tot sententiæ.* But nowadays we ought to widen the aphorism; for not only is there an utter disagreement among individuals, but moreover, on examining the several conceptions held by the same individual, it will be found, as a rule, that these conceptions are radically incompatible one with another. There cannot be a doubt that some doctrine is urgently required which may put an end to this lamentable state of things,—this disorder so unworthy of organic men.

—————ooo—————

I.—MISCELLANEOUS ARTICLES.

1.—THE IMPORTANCE OF POSITIVISM, AND THE PREPARATION NECESSARY FOR THE STUDY OF IT. *

POSITIVISM, as a system of philosophy, is now gaining great influence in Europe. Within a few years it has passed far beyond the narrow limits it had attained during the life-time of its founder†—the little band of early disciples has grown into a large and powerful school, the scorn of foes has been converted into respect, a general curiosity has been awakened, and no book on philosophy is considered complete which does not contain some estimate of Positivism. Little, however, is known of the labours of Comte in India‡ : for the educated natives of this country, Hamilton and Mill are, as a rule, the two great exponents of modern European thought. The other thinkers whom India delights to honour are but the satellites which cluster round these two great luminaries. Now, Hamilton and Mill, opposed as they are to each other, both agree in maintaining the fruitfulness of metaphysical speculation. Comte on the other hand always consistently maintained the utter futility and barrenness of such in-

* This article is a combination of two which appeared in the Bengalee:— the first on Aug. 3. 1867, the second on Oct. 2. 1867. The article of Aug. 3, 1867, was the first which appeared, in the columns of the Bengalee, on the subject of Positivism.

† Comte died in 1857.

‡ This was written more than two years ago. It cannot be said now that Positivism is unknown in Bengal; though, as a rule, it is far from being correctly appreciated or thoroughly understood.

vestigations. Discarding all enquiry as to first or final causes he limits the human mind to a less ambitious but more remunerative task, *viz.*—to the discovery of how phenomena are related to each other. At first such discovery may seem but a poor result, yet when we remember that the knowledge which it involves endows man with foresight, and enables him to exercise a vast power of control over surrounding circumstances, we cannot fail to acknowledge that it is pregnant with the most important consequences. The simple staff which Positive Science has given man to lean upon, becomes a magician's wand conferring on its possessor the most signal advantages, and enabling him so to regulate his destiny as to do away hereafter with much of the evil and misery which now afflict the world.

The metaphysicians of Europe can teach no new lessons to those who in their Sanskrit lore can find systems as daring and fascinating as any that have been elaborated by western thinkers. The Hindoo mind still revels, as of old, in *a priori* speculations, still delights to construct an unstable fabric of knowledge on a purely subjective basis. It seems to us that a corrective is urgently needed, in the present age, for this metaphysical tendency which is so natural to the Hindoo mind : and such a corrective we believe will be afforded by a careful study of Positivism.

These who take an interest in such subjects are strongly advised to have recourse to the fountain-head, in order that they may judge for themselves how far Comte has made good his claim to inaugurate a new era in the history of the human mind : an era, however, which he regards as the logical result of the past, each of the previous stages being absolutely essential in order to constitute the final one.

In commencing the study of Positivism, a difficulty may be experienced at the outset in fully mastering the scientific conceptions which form the basis upon which the whole system rests. The difficulty is undeniable, but its magnitude may be, and generally is, much exaggerated. A certain mental cultivation is desirable; a knowledge, for instance, of the elements of mathematics, an acquaintance with the general facts of history, and some few leading notions regarding the chief inductive sciences. These requirements are possessed at present by most educated men, but where they do not exist a special, though not prolonged, training will be necessary in order to secure them.

The fundamental scientific conceptions are not numerous, and may be soon mastered by any one of ordinary intelligence. The knowledge required is neither minute nor encyclopædic; it is not necessary to trace any one of the sciences through all its complicated details, nor is it necessary to study all or any large number of those subjects which are usually termed scientific. As a mere tyro in Mathematics can be made to appreciate the law of gravitation without wading through the whole of Newton's Principia, so a person of very meagre scientific attainments can form a fair estimate of Comte's Philosophy without putting himself through a preliminary course of training in some encyclopædia of modern science.

The scale of abstract sciences as given by Comte, consists of seven degrees. First, *Mathematics* which deals with Number, Extension, and Motion, attributes common to all things. Secondly, *Astronomy* which deals with the *geometrical* and *mechanical* relations of the earth to the other stars. Thirdly, *Physics*, which deals with what metaphysicians term the secondary qualities of matter, as weight, heat, sound, colour, electricity, and magnetism. Fourthly, *Chemistry*, which deals with the molecular constitution of bodies. Fifthly, *Biology*, which deals with the general study of life in all its forms. Sixthly, *Sociology*, which deals with society. Seventhly, *Morals*, which deals with man as an individual.

The arrangement here adopted is so natural and so simple that it needs no explanation in order to impress it upon the mind. A single glance will show that the subjects are arranged, in an ascending order, according to their increasing complexity and the decreasing generality of the phenomena dealt with. The order given can be verified by showing that it accords with the actual order of development in history.*

This classification must be thoroughly mastered, and certain leading scientific principles must be acquired for this purpose. Owing to our too strictly literary education there are many not fully qualified to undertake such a task, with the slender stock of science they have brought from the schools. When education is placed upon a sounder basis, this deficiency will, in a great measure, disappear : in the meanwhile Positivism must appeal for a hearing simply to those who are duly prepared intellectually, and to those who are willing to undertake the not very formidable labour required for mastering the few fundamental conceptions connected with the subjects above enumerated.

An acquaintance with Arithmetic and Geometry, and with Mechanics, so far as to appreciate thoroughly the three Laws of Motion, will be found, if not quite sufficient, at least highly valuable, wherever the principles of science and the operations of the human mind, in the discovery of the laws of nature, are involved. The history and theory of Astronomy, as contained in any good popular treatise, should be read : and an attempt should be made to learn the rudiments of Chemistry and Physiology, no gigantic task in the present age when the materials for accomplishing it

* This statement must not be interpreted too literally. It can only be appreciated fully by those who have thoroughly mastered Comte's *Positive Philosophy* and the volume on History in the *Politique Positive*. Our fundamental conceptions have in fact advanced simultaneously though at different rates. During the advance each conception has acted upon all the others, being in its turn reacted upon by those others—the actions and re-actions, at each epoch, depending upon the then state of the general body of scientific conceptions.

exist in such abundance. It may be presumed that in general no special training beyond that of the schools will be required for History ; but it must not be forgotten that the wider and deeper the historical researches have been, the more prepared will the student find himself for appreciating the triumphs of Comte, which are most signal in the field of History.

———————ooo———————

2.—THE ABSTRACT SCIENCES FORM A NATURAL SCALE.*

MATHEMATICS is the basis upon which all the higher sciences rest, and without which they could not exist. Neither Astronomy nor Physics could advance a single step without the aid of Arithmetic and Geometry. Chemistry in like manner cannot dispense with the aid of Physics ; and without Chemistry nutrition, which is the foundation of all vital energy, would be perfectly unintelligible. Lastly, an exact theory of life is required in order to secure a stable foundation for Sociology or the History of man's collective development.

A general glance at the objects which surround us is sufficient to disclose among them certain natural divisions and marked characteristics. The organic world is manifestly separate and distinct from the inorganic, the latter being, as it were, a particular case of the former, and necessary for its existence. A limited portion of matter only is susceptible of organisation and life, and this portion while it obeys the special laws of life, at the same time obeys the more general laws which regulate all physical phenomena—being influenced by chemical affinity, electricity, heat, and weight. It is important to observe that among the great variety of known elements there are but few which, by their combination, can give rise to organic life. The chief are oxygen, hydrogen, azote, and

---

* These remarks are taken from a small pamphlet, by M. Littre, entitled, *Paroles de Philosophie Positive.*

carbon, with which a few others such as phosphorus, iron, sodium, &c., are conjoined. Thus life is characterised not only by certain special properties, but also by requiring for its development a special combination of elementary substances.

Again the vegetative life which characterises the vegetable world, which is the basis of all animal life, and which consists in a perpetual recurrence of composition and decompsition, must depend intimately upon those molecular actions and re-actions which are termed *chemical*. Vital phenomena presuppose chemical phenomena ; wherever the former are found there are also the latter, but the latter are not necessarily accompanied by the former. Hence chemical properties rank next below those which are peculiar to organised bodies. *Every* substance is susceptible of chemical action, on which account chemical phenomena are rightly classed among those which are general. But though general yet in each case of chemical action a *specific* difference is found. In order to produce chemical phenomena it is requisite that *two* different substances or elements should be brought into immediate contact : a couple, or binary combination, is in all cases essential. Thus in chemistry as well as in physiology a special combination of substances is required to develope a peculiar class of properties.

Again physical properties must, according to the order of complexity, rank below chemical properties. The problems dealt with in physics have reference to the masses, and not, as in chemistry, to the constituent molecules of bodies. The properties investigated are those of weight, elasticity, heat, sound, light, colour, and electricity. These are more general than chemical properties since they require no contact between the substances : they manifest themselves as well when bodies are in a state of isolation as when they are combined: a pure metal, such as gold, and a pure gas, such as oxygen, manifest in themselves no chemical property, but are each endowed with physical properties. Hence we have a descending scale of phenomena, vital, chemical and physical ; and below these, forming as it were the basis on which the whole superstructure rests, are number, space, and time, which give rise to mathematics.

To recapitulate. Number, space, and time, constitute the basis of all knowledge and give rise to mathematics the most elementary and most general of all the sciences. Next in an ascending scale come physical properties, which are strictly general, being found in all substances whether separate or combined. As we advance the phenomena become more special, the next in order of complexity being those of chemistry which require a definite combination of elements to develope those peculiar molecular actions which are termed chemical. Advancing still higher we at length arrive at vital properties which are still more special, and which can only be developed by combinations formed from a very limited number of elementary substances.

———ooo———

3.—POSITIVISM SOMETHING MORE THAN A SYSTEMATISATION OF SCIENCE.

THE student should not be discouraged, at the outset, by the dry and uninviting details with which Positivism appears to abound. The scientific facts and conceptions which are so constantly appealed to, form but the rude scaffolding behind which a new and beautiful fabric lies concealed. This fabric is not simply another shrine erected for the glorification of modern science, but a temple at whose altars refuge may be found from much of the discord and misery which now afflict mankind. Positivism does not limit itself to the improvement of science ; it has a loftier ambition, a nobler aim. It claims to be an inheritor of no mean share in the rich

legacy of good left to the human race by the great and
virtuous in all ages.   It even appeals to its adversaries,
who are likewise engaged in the task of social ameli-
oration, to co-operate with it in diminishing the sum
of human evil, and in endeavouring to inaugurate a
happier era when

> This earth shall be the Paradise
> It never look'd to human eyes
> Since Adam left his garden yet.

To many it may appear that such hopes are visionary,
such plans chimerical.   But can any one doubt that
the intellectual condition of most educated men,
throughout the civilized world, is now fraught with
danger to themselves, and, should it continue, with
serious injury to posterity?   Indecision, selfishness, im-
morality, and mental despair, are some of the evils
which result from the prevailing negativism of the
present age.   The orthodox teachers are not listened to,
preach they never so wisely.   There seems to be a latent conviction that such teachers are rather advocates
struggling to prop up a dying cause, than ardent evangelists proclaiming a living truth which is good for
all men.

Positivism under such circumstances simply asks for
a hearing, in hopes that when other remedies have
failed it may furnish an antidote to the malady.
Though it discards the search for the unknown, none
can say that its human ideal is not a lofty one.   Its
gospel is that of Humanity, it proclaims peace
and good-will to all men, it enforces the dignity of
human labour and substitutes the calm heroism of
peaceful industry for the ruthless energy of armed bat-
talions; it aspires to replace selfishness by devotion,
rights by duties, anarchy by order, and it looks forward
hopefully to a brighter day when the human race shall
rest at length from all the weary suffering of the past,
while

....the war-drum throbs no longer, and the battle-flags are furl'd,
In the Parliament of man, the Federation of the world.

4.—CASTE.

THOSE reformers who are, nowadays, in the habit of describing Caste as the source of all the evils and disorders which can be traced in Hindoo Society, forget apparently the very important services which it has rendered to mankind in the past, and quite overlook the impossibility of completely uprooting an institution which has taken such a firm hold on the popular mind. They seem to regard the present state of society in Europe as the ideal of perfection, whereas that state is altogether transitory and is symptomatic rather of disease than of health. A painful life of unremunerated toil among large classes, a rebellion against anything that savours of organisation or control, a morbid craving to rise ever higher in the social scale, a desperate struggle on the part of each man to outrun his neighbours in the wild chase after wealth and honours—these and their results are not to be regarded as the normal conditions of Humanity. Yet a state of society in which these are the prevailing characteristics is being continually held up to the admiration of Eastern nations as the last result of time, the *ne plus ultra* of social and political organisation.

The attempt to abolish caste, if successful, would be attended with the most dangerous consequences unless some powerful religious influences were brought to bear upon the people at large, so that the old bonds might be replaced by others of equal strength if of a less objectionable nature. The Brahmos perhaps would assert that they are prepared with a suitable remedy for any evils that might arise from tampering with the long established prejudices of the people. We have grave doubts as to the efficacy of their antidote. Past experience does not warrant the conclusion that Brahmoism can present any formidable barrier to the daring scepticism and crude commercial spirit of the present age. Its metaphysical dogmas may captivate minds of a certain type, but these dogmas must undergo a vast modification before they can exercise a powerful influence upon the people at large.*

The most able men among the new school of reformers are devoid of any definite religious belief, and apparently they are not as yet prepared to suggest any means of carrying their schemes into effect in such a manner as to neutralise the dangers to which we have above alluded. They simply advocate the wholesale importation, among their countrymen, of European civilisation in its most material and anarchical forms, without any moral safeguards. We think that the wiser plan would be that they should wait till the West itself is more settled before they apply its modes of thought and action, on any large scale, to a community which is not as yet prepared to assimilate them.

It may be said,—If, in introducing European civilisation, you require moral safeguards, why not at once recommend the adoption of Christianity. Our answer is as follows :—

The religion of the future, whatever form it may assume, must spring up as the natural consequence of the nation's past history and present organisation, and cannot be introduced wholly from without. The annals of missionary enterprise have shown clearly enough that a new and foreign creed can be imposed upon a community only when its state of civilisation is most rudimentary, and when the popular mind is still impregnated with a rude fetichism which easily gives place to a more organic form of belief. Christianity

---

* We allude here to Brahmoism in its older form. The so-called Progressive Brahmoism is too recent to enable us to pronounce any very definite opinion as to its merits. The *leaders* of the movement are capable men it may be, but neither Pauls nor Gautamas. Some of the schemes which they put most prominently forward do not appear calculated to win the masses, while they are certain to alienate the higher classes of their fellow-countrymen. The *followers* (if we may credit newspaper-gossip) are for the most part simple enthusiasts whose religious conceptions can scarcely be supposed to shed much lustre upon the Church to which they belong.

in this country must fail to spread, because it is confronted with a system resting upon foundations not dissimilar to its own, and so plastic that it can be moulded into the most diverse forms—adapting itself equally to the intellect of the subtle metaphysician and the emotions of the unlettered peasant. Hindoo Polytheism, however, in spite of its metaphysical subtlety and wide range of influence, is, we are willing to admit, now in a state of decay. But it must be replaced by a religion which shall reflect the national life while having its roots in man's moral nature, and not by some exotic system devoid of all vivifying power, and utterly incompetent to form a nucleus round which the love and reverence of its votaries may cluster.

With reference to Caste, our advice would be,—modify, but do not destroy it; let its distinctive conceptions be preserved, but let them gradually be placed upon a social instead of a supernatural basis. The problem may be a difficult one, but in proportion to its difficulty will be the merit and the reward of those who succeed in solving it; certainly there is neither difficulty nor merit in the present mode of procedure, which is merely a cutting of the Gordian knot. We shall now present our readers with an appreciation of the caste system from the Positivist point of view.

Historically it will be found that the institution of caste occurs among all populations at a certain stage of their development: it is everywhere one of the essential features of Polytheism in its theocratic phase. The Hellenic and Latin races were at one time subject to it, though at the dawn of what is called the historical period the traces of its influence are beginning to disappear. The local causes which favored its growth, and which, in many cases, have rendered it permanent till now, were—according to Comte—" a combination of a fine climate with a fertile soil favoring intellectual development by making subsistence easy; a territory admitting naturally of internal communication; and a country so isolated as to be secure from invasion, while offering no strong inducements to a life of war." Speaking of the *natural origin* of caste, Comte says :— " The universality and tenacity of the sytem are a sufficient proof of its suitability to human needs, in its season, notwithstanding the inconveniences it involved. Nothing, indeed, could be more natural, at the outset, than that, by domestic imitation,—the easiest and most powerful means of education,—employments should descend from fathers to sons : and it was the *only possible* training in an age when oral transmission was the sole means of communicating conceptions. In fact, there is, and always will be, a tendency to the hereditary adoption of employments, however different the modern method may be from the ancient. When men have no special impulse to a particular occupation, they naturally adopt that of the family.

In describing its *properties*, he says :—" We owe to it the first permanent division between Theory and Practice, by the institution of a speculative class, invested with grand prerogatives of dignity and leisure: and to this period we must refer the primitive elements of genuine Knowledge,—it being that in which the human mind began to regulate its general course. The same may be said of the Fine Arts, then carefully cultivated, not only for the sake of their charm, but as tributary to dogma and worship on the one hand, and information and religious propagation on the other. The Industrial development was the most remarkable of all, requiring no rare intellectual qualifications, inspiring no fear in the ruling class, and furnishing, under the reign of peace, forces adequate to the most colossal undertakings. The loss of many useful inventions before the preservative institution of caste arose must have suggested the need of it, and have proved its advantages afterwards in securing the division of labour which was here and there attained. No institution has ever shown itself more adapted to honour ability of various kinds than this polytheistic organisation, which often exalted into apotheosis its commemoration of eminent inventors, who were offered to the adoration of their respective castes. In a social view, the virtues of the system are not less conspicuous. Politically, its chief attribute was stability. All precautions against attack from within and from without were most energetically instituted. Within, all the castes were united by the single bond of their common subordination to the sacerdotal caste from which each derived all that it had of special knowledge and perpetual instigation. There never was elsewhere such a concentration, for intensity, regularity, and permanence of human power, as that possessed by the supreme caste, each member of which, (at least, in the higher ranks of the priesthood,) was not only priest and magistrate, but also philosopher, artist, engineer, and physician. * * * As to the influence on Morals, this system was favourable to *personal* morality, and yet more to domestic, for the spirit of caste was a mere extension of the family spirit. The condition of women was improved, notwithstanding the prevalence of polygamy; for they were rescued from the subjection to rude toil which had been their lot in a barbaric age; and their seclusion, according to the customs of polygamy, was the first token of homage, and of their assignment to a position more conformable to their true nature. As to *social* morals,— the system was evidently favorable to respect for age, and homage to ancestors. The sentiment of patriotism did not as yet transcend love of caste, which, narrow as it appears to us, was a necessary preparation for the higher attachment."

The above estimate may perhaps serve towards a more correct appreciation of the caste system than that which is generally held at the present time by most amateur and not a few professed politicians. To the student of history we especially recommend it, and we trust that it may have some influence in redeeming a noble institution from the undeserved contempt with which it is too often regarded.

———ooo———

5.—FATHER HYACINTHE.

THE Protestant press of England has welcomed with loud tumult of acclaim the letter in which Father Hyacinthe makes known, to his own Superior and to the world at large, his secession from the Order of Barefooted Carmelites. On the banks of the Thames the eloquent preacher of Notre Dame is praised beyond measure for his courage and enlightenment, while the Church of Rome is overwhelmed with censure for its bigotry and crude despotism. The French press, on the other hand, while acknowledging the importance of the event, is not so unanimous in conceding unmixed praise to Father Hyacinthe. In France, it is seen clearly that the appeal to individual conscience, if made consistently, would lead the appellant much farther than to a simple protest aginst " doctrines and practices which are called Roman, but which are not Christian." For such an appeal must lead ultimately to a total abandonment of dogmatic Christianity, whether in its Catholic or Protestant form, and to an enlistment under the banners of Freethought, where alone the claims of the *individual* and of the *general* conscience can be fully reconciled. This result which is only timidly hinted at by certain organs of the English press, is openly and emphatically proclaimed by almost the whole of the non-Catholic portion of the French press. Everywhere but in England, it is fearlessly maintained by the party of progress that the great religious contest of the present century is between Catholicism and Freethought, and not between Catholicism and Protestantism. The sooner England too comes to recognise this frankly, the better will it be for the welfare of mankind; for the public opinion of England is a very potent element in modern civilisation, owing to the facility with which it can be manifested, and the ample means which exist for circulating it when formed. While England stands aloof as now from the liberal party on the Continent, the attempt to bring about a better state of things is seriously impeded.

The step taken by Father Hyacinthe is not one of any new or peculiar significance. The growing divergence between the policy of Rome and what is termed the spirit of the Age, is not a thing of yesterday. It is a subject which has especially agitated the minds of churchmen in France ever since the downfal of the first Napoleon. It was upon this rock that the gifted Lamennais split, and the noble Lacordaire was nearly wrecked. This happened more than thirty years ago, and at the same time many of the most eminent Catholics in France were sadly perplexed between their allegiance to Rome and their attachment to what they regarded as the sacred cause of Freedom. It was a trying period for the Papacy, as all parties looked to it for a solution of the pending difficulties while it was inevitable that some should be disappointed. The storm however was not unsuccessfully weathered, and Catholicism still remains erect and strengthened—as compared with her old adversaries, the sects of Protestantism.

Father Hyacinthe, it would seem, has not yet decided upon his final course of action. If he is consistent, only two alternatives are open to him; either, like Lamennais, to ally himself frankly with the modern movement, (stigmatised by Rome as the Revolution); or, like Lacordaire, to submit unreservedly to the Papal authority. Rome, as he must well know, will accept no half allegiance; and, as a Frenchman, he cannot hesitate about the course he should adopt when once he has abandoned Catholicism.

The struggle now taking place between Catholic conservatism and European progress is an important one. It has reference not so much to dogma, as to the ge-

neral mode of thought and regimen of life. Everywhere men, while retaining the old watchwords, are
profoundly modifying the conceptions which these
wachwords involved and the institutions which clus-
tered round them. Among the growing beliefs, may
be reckoned a conviction that the present fusion between the spiritual and the temporal is not destined
to be permanent, that a new order of things must eventually be established—in which government shall rest
upon a purely civil basis, and religion shall be left to
the free play of man's intellectual and moral forces.
There is little fear nowadays of any aggression on the
part of the spiritual power; the danger is rather in the
other direction, that the temporal power should be
tempted to interfere in matters which are not purely
practical—as for instance when the State allies itself
with Universities and learned Societies, thereby giving
certain favored cliques a fictitious advantage in the
struggle for intellectual dominion. In order that the
separation between the two powers may be complete the
State must confine itself solely to the functions of practical government, and must leave both Science and
Religion to take care of themselves.*

That Rome with all its glories is doomed to become
a mere historical recollection, we—as believers in the
ever-onward progress of our race—regard as not admitting of a doubt. But her empire will not pass away
till she has fought many another stern battle with the
forces of Liberalism; and when the last traces of her
temporal power have disappeared, we may expect that
she will reign with increased vigor in the hearts of her
best and sincerest followers. The temporal power, however necessary and beneficial it may have been to the
Church at one time, is now a fatal boon; for it seriously clogs her freedom in all transactions with the Kings†

---

* This of course only applies to communities which have reached a certain
stage of intellectual and political advancement.

† The term ' Kings' must here be understood in a general sense. The modern conflict is between the Few and the Many, between the old *feudal* and
the new *industrial* spirit.

on the one side, and with the peoples on the other. As a sovereign power she cannot ally herself with the people against the kings; as the champion of the poor and the oppressed, she ought not to be a silent witness to the suffering of the many and the insolent triumph of the few. Yet whichever side she espouses, the alliance in either case is likely to prove equally dangerous—the kings are almost certain to be insincere friends, and the peoples, even if willing to yield in the matter of dogmatic beliefs, would allow no tampering with their political and social programme. Were Rome not hampered with any temporal sovereignty her position as a mediator between contending powers would be much improved: for she could then be perfectly neutral, and her admonitions would be listened to with respect even in quarters where they would not be welcomed as proceeding from a wisdom that cannot err. But she has decided that the temporal power which she now holds, is essential to her well-being if not to her existence, and after the Revolution of July 1830, she definitively allied herself with the kings against the peoples, with the old order against the new. The result of her policy has been to create a re-action in her favour among the aristocratic classes, but to alienate for ever the generous impulses of the democracy. The lip-service of the upper classes is however but a doubtful benefit, and will not compensate her for the ingratitude of kings and governments, whose cause she so nobly defended in the hour of their supreme peril.

The subdued conflict which may be observed within the Catholic Church itself, between the Papal power on the one side and the Episcopacy on the other, cannot be regarded as any sign of weakness or decay. It is a conflict which has lasted for centuries, and which will doubtless continue as long as the Church itself. A similar conflict must go on, under some form or other, in every organised society, between the aristocratic and dictatorial elements, between those who occupy positions of authority all but the highest, and the individual or individuals to whom are entrusted the highest functions of command.

————ooo————

6.—UTILITARIANISM.

It will be found that the arguments urged by utilitarians against the objections of their opponents, almost invariably rest upon a single principle, namely, That it is possible to effect an absolute separation between the *test* and the *source* of morality. We refuse to admit that such a separation is a valid one. The question of the *test* really involves that of the *source*, so that the two cannot be distinguished except for logical purposes. And even when they are distinguished in thought, it must always be borne in mind that in practice they are intimately combined. When utilitarians assert that an action is virtuous *because* it is useful, they implicitly confound virtue with utility. For, (assuming that virtue and utility have only a *relative* existence,) the utilitarian rule necessarily involves the position, that our notion of virtue depends upon our notion of utility. Now admitting this dependence, it follows that utility is the antecedent and virtue the consequent, that the notion of utility springs up first in the mind and gives rise subsequently to the notion of virtue. The notion of utility thus becomes the primary and fundamental one, or, in other words, utility is the *source* as well as the *test* of virtue.

It will hence appear that there is a vast difference between the two propositions, (1) Virtuous actions conduce to the public welfare, and (2) Actions are virtuous *because* they conduce to the public welfare. The first of these we willingly admit, the second involves a sophism which is likely to give rise to injurious results in practice. According to the first duty and happiness simply coincide, according to the second duty is nothing more than an ignominious fiction.

Utilitarians, if we understand them aright, appear

to think it highly advantageous that men should aq able to *prove* what is right. Now although morality undoubtedly rests upon a rational basis, yet in practice Feeling must always predominate over Reason. The encroachments of the Intellect on the domain of morals should be very carefully watched. In the majority of cases that occur we are not called upon to decide anew what is right. The moral code has been determined for us by the gradual and painful development of the race, and we have simply now to obey its precepts. In the formation of character we should set before ourselves the brightest and best exemplars of Humanity in the past, and model our conduct upon theirs. In such books as the Bible, the Koran, the Confessions of S. Augustine, the Imitation of Christ, —there can be found moral precepts and moral ideals, which if carefully studied will enable us altogether to dispense with the dubious doctrines of our modern utilitarian evangelists. The foundation of Right is Duty. Our various duties have been slowly developed. They are well-defined now, and each one should be trained from youth to observe them, so that there be no need for hesitation in the emergencies of every-day life. The moral education of the individual is, and ever must be, performed in the home and by the mother. It is the mother who instils into the mind of the child all those moral prejudices which have grown up with the growth of the race. The child thus goes through, in a few years, a process which it has taken the race many centuries to accomplish. In this training the intellect plays a very minor part. Attachment, obedience, trust, and such-like feelings, are those which are chiefly called into action. It should be the principal aim of practical morality to intensify and regulate this early education so as to connect Virtue immediately with Feeling, and circumscribe within as narrow limits as possible the office of the Intellect.

The utilitarian asserts that an impulse is *virtuous* if

the tendency of such an impulse can be shown to make the individual a happy man, and to make him a useful member of society. Now, assuming that we are dealing with one who denies the existence of an inherent tendency to virtue, does this mean that an individual,—having only certain impulses towards the attainment of happiness,—when convinced that, by a certain course of action, he himself or the community will be benefited, not only decides upon gratifying this happiness-seeking impulse, but affixes to it a new name and calls it *virtuous?* If so, why this new name, why is the impulse *virtuous* as well as *utilitarian?* Surely the term *virtuous*, upon such an hypothesis, is altogether surperfluous, and men might as well be told plainly that Humanity, in past times, has been troubling itself very unnecessarily in coining a double vocabulary when a single one would have served equally well.

The utilitarian sometimes argues that utility must be the test of morality because the moral codes of different nations agree only upon those points which involve the well-being of mankind. But men could not have been guided solely by utility in framing these codes. We can see *now* that they agree in those measures which are conducive to man's welfare. It could not have been foreseen, in early times, if indeed the problem could have been stated, what would be the points in which the codes of different nations would eventually agree. Each nation did the best it could according to the light which was in it, and a process of very gradual development has at last brought into prominence those principles which were permanent and beneficial. But this very fact,—that as we narrow our point of view, and confine ourselves to some special nation or tribe, influences come into play which the utilitarian theory cannot explain,—shows evidently enough that utility has not been the antecedent principle, the impelling force. Societies have been formed because there is in man a spontaneous tendency to sociability: utility on a grand scale has been elaborated only after many painful experiments and partial failures.

The rules of life, as we now have them, have been the result of a long and gradual process of development. At the commencement they must have been determined not by the consequences of actions, but by certain spontaneous tendencies in man himself. Take for instance *monogamy*. How could it have been discovered beforehand that the happiness resulting from having one wife would, on the whole, be greater than the happiness resulting from having two or more? Such a discovery was manifestly impossible. Either then the rise of monogamy was altogether accidental, and men continued to practise it because they found that certain beneficial consequences resulted from this accidental arrangement; or, if it was not accidental, those who first adopted it could not have been impelled by utilitarian principles, because its utility could not *then* have been manifest.

If the ancient Romans had made happiness or utility the test of their conduct, they surely would never have undertaken those vast military enterprises which always brought misery to individuals and often extensive injury to the state, but which have been the means of conferring incalculable blessings upon their successors—blessings which could not, in ancient times, have been even dimly foreseen. Had they guided their actions simply by the maxims of utility they would no doubt have preferred a peaceful existence, and Humanity would never have advanced beyond the theocratic stage. A principle which is thus contradicted by the laws of human nature two thousand years ago, cannot be in accordance with those laws at the present time. Hence the proposition—*That Utility is the test of virtue*—cannot be regarded as one that gives anything like a correct view. Positivism sums up the whole of sound morality in its maxim *Live for others*; and rightly so, because Humanity has always been tending towards altruism, all history being but a record of the gradual triumph of the social and benevolent elements in our nature over those which are purely selfish and personal. But as the solution of the moral problem is a progressive one, it is only in these latter times that the maxim has become thoroughly realisable. It could not be even formulated until there were sufficient data at hand upon which to found a correct conclusion as to the real nature of human perfection. Any sound moral rule ought to fulfil two requisities : (1) It should contain nothing which contradicts the tendencies of human nature at any period of man's history, and (2) It should sum up in a few words that course of action which results from a perfect development of all our faculties. The rule of Positivism satisfies both these conditions ; the rule of Utilitarianism certainly violates the first. It may be here observed that the moral rules of any given period in the past will be those which correspond to the highest possible development of that period. Such rules must be modified with the gradual progress of the race.

Great stress is laid by utilitarians on the separation between actions and agents. Language is sometimes used which would induce one to suppose that these theorists believe in actions as separate entities, existing like Plato's *ideas* in an archetypal world of their own. What, let us ask, does any general moral rule imply? Simply this, that in the greater number of instances that can occur it will be right to follow the rule. Cases of course may occur in which the rule ought not to be obeyed, but such cases may be regarded as purely exceptional. The rule then has no significance *per se*, it merely indicates what impulse ought to be followed by agents in the great majority of circumstances that will present themselves in practice. It leaves out of view the exceptions, because to lay stress upon them might impair the force of the general precept, and produce confusion in the minds of the agents to whom they are addressed. The popular logic very soon arrived at the conclusion, That every rule must have its exceptions; but the popular intellect was instinctively conscious that, in the rules of morality, the exceptions were of minor importance.

To illustrate these remarks, let us examine some general precept—*Thou shalt not steal*, for example. How is such a rule arrived at? We believe that the process is somewhat as follows. Man is endowed with an industrial or constructive instinct which leads him to accumulate wealth. He spontaneouly exercises this instinct, and in order to do so with success a necessary condition is, that A should not be allowed, with impunity, to deprive B by violence or fraud of that property which B may have gained without the exercise of violence or fraud. As our development advances, the classification of our instincts is gradually systematised—some are felt to be more dignified than others, and to such an exalted rank and honorable name are assigned; they are termed *moral*, and give rise to moral rules. The instinct in question, namely that of construction, is placed at the head of our egoistic instincts, and with reference to it the moral rule *Thou shalt not steal* is formulated. This rule is an advertisement to all future individuals and generations of the part played by the constructive instinct in the development of the race.

The utilitarian theory of life is thus stated by Mr. J. S. Mill—"Pleasure, and freedom from pain, are the only things desirable as ends; and all desirable things are desirable either for the pleasure inherent in themselves, or as means to the promotion of pleasure and the prevention of pain." As Mr. Mill very justly observes, "such a theory of life excites in many minds, and among them in some of the most estimable in feeling and purpose, inveterate dislike." We are well aware that very happy consequences are deduced by Mr. Mill from the somewhat repulsive formula above given. He tells us that utilitarian pleasures include "pleasures of the intellect, of the feelings and imagination, and of the moral sentiments." It would have been perhaps as well if some indication of this comprehensive use of the term pleasure had been given in the formula itself. Human nature must undergo a very radical change before the generality of men can be induced to regard such a term as otherwise than highly objectionable when employed to indicate the end, the *summum bonum* of man's existence. Would not any one who simply knew the enunciation of the utilitarian theory of life—and most men know no more—be startled at the unexpected consequences which Mr. Mill has deduced from it? Is it not a fact that every student of morals, when he first directs his attention to utilitarianism, is surprised to find that a doctrine which proclaims pleasure to be the end of life can be converted into a means for the general cultivation of nobleness of character, and for the promotion of the highest interests of Humanity?

What would ordinary men be inclined to make of such a theory? It is neatly stated and dwells easily in the memory. Would they hedge it in with all the precautions which Mr. Mill has adopted? Would they not inevitably, *as individuals*, make such a rule bend to their own interests and enjoyments? Of course there will be bad men under any system, men who will violate or pervert the best of rules. But is this rule stated in terms likely to command the self sacrifice of the individual, to make him study his own welfare simply through the welfare of others—not indeed to neglect himself, but to regard all self-improvement from a social point of view, to remember constantly that he is one of a vast community which extends throughout all time, and that we are all of us, as St. Paul has so inimitably expressed it, "members one of another"?

It is the dangerous language of utilitarianism that forms one of its most objectionable features. This is a point on which mere discussion avails nothing. If the danger is not *felt*, the intellect alone will not enable us to discern it. Because Bentham, Mill and others have deduced very valuable consequences from very repulsive principles, it does not follow that men in general will do the same. The probability is, that those who accept the principles will deduce from them such consequences as may be pleasing in their own sight.

II.—REVIEWS.

1.—RATIONALISM AND FAITH.

A SERIES of articles, contributed not long ago to the columns of the *Indo-European Correspondence*, have been lately republished in the form of a pamphlet. The articles are preceded by a somewhat elaborate preface in which the merits of Catholicism are eloquently advocated, while its rational basis is most satisfactorily laid down. The pamphlet is entitled "Rationalism and Faith."

We believe this little volume is calculated to do much good by drawing the attention of Bengalee students of history to the part played by Catholicism in the civilisation of the world. It is not our object to uphold Catholicism as a definitive creed or as adapted to the wants of the present century, but we are decidedly of opinion that it is, and has been, too much the fashion in this country altogether to ignore the power of a system which moulded the infant communities of modern Europe, which provided a worship and a discipline under which the most advanced nations lived and flourished for more than ten centuries, and which —though its dream of universal power has been for ever dissipated—has sought and found enthusiastic votaries in every region of the globe.

We can only ascribe the unreasonable contempt for Catholicism, which we have observed among the educated classes in India, to the essentially Protestant bias received in early life, at school or college. The scheme of education, hitherto adopted, has not enforced Christianity it is true, but yet it has succeeded in communicating to the youth of India the strongest prejudices of Protestantism—and it *has* thus succeeded simply because no compulsion of any kind has been at work, the process having been an unconscious one; but all

the more disastrous on this very account, the difficulty
of recalling the mind to a better state, being increased a
hundred-fold by the absence of any *reasoned* opinions or
convictions which have resulted from a mental conflict.
A vague kind of half rational, half evangelical Protestantism has hitherto tinged almost all the history and
a considerable portion of the English literature taught in
India; the faintest possible opportunity has thus been afforded to native students for arriving at an impartial view
of the religious growth and spiritual life of modern Europe: hence too the doctrines of Reformation, though
not accepted by the educated Hindoo as guides in matters of religion, may nevertheless be regarded as having powerfully influenced the whole tenour of his
thought. We have often been surprised indeed to find
how readily the popular objections to Catholicism are
caught up, and how tenaciously they are adhered to by
men of considerable intellectual attainments, and who,
as Hindoos, can have no personal interest in adopting
one point of view rather than another. Even those
men in the Universities who graduate in Honors, are
fortunate if the lessons taught them by Guizot or Hal-
lam have partially succeeded in modifying their earlier
opinions. Such books as Bossuet's 'History of Protestant Variations,' his 'Exposition of Catholic Doctrine,'
De Maistre on 'The Pope,' and Chateaubriand's 'Genius of Christianity,' are we believe not among those
which are prescribed by the Calcutta University, nor
among those which are generally recommended for
private perusal. Yet these and others of their kind
ought to be read, if an impartial opinion is to be formed of European history.

But though demanding a fair hearing for Catholicism, we would have it distinctly understood that, in
our opinion, neither Catholicism nor any other form
of Theology will eventually succeed in winning the
intellectual assent of mankind. According to the author of 'Rationalism and Faith,' Christianity prophe-

cies that as knowledge increases faith will diminish—it may be so, but Christianity can hardly blame the infidel for fulfilling her own prophecies. The historian Gibbon tells us, in his own playful semi-orthodox way, that the brave and impetuous Clovis, when he heard "the pathetic tale of the passion and death of Christ exclaimed, with indiscreet fury, 'Had I been present at the head of my valiant Franks, I would have revenged his injuries,' thus forgetting in his generous passion *the salutary consequences of that mysterious sacrifice.*" In the same way we too might remind the elect, when they censure the sceptic and the atheist, that they do not sufficiently weigh the salutary consequences that must result from the accomplishment of Prophecy. Let us proceed, however, to more serious considerations. Our modern instinct as we believe, condemns many of the fundamental dogmas upon which Christianity is founded, dogmas which are not brought into prominence in such controversial books as the one we are now reviewing, but which have great influence on the decisions of those who are altogether outside the pale of Christianity. The following are the dogmas to which we more especially allude, (1) That the benevolent instincts are foreign to our nature, (2) That labour is the result of the Divine curse, (3) That woman is the source of all evil. But we are willing to admit that "the wisdom of the Catholic priesthood, aided by a favorable situation, was able during several centuries to check the natural evils of such doctrines, so as to draw from them, provisionally, admirable results for society."* Nevertheless "during the three centuries of its rise to power Christianity never failed to elicit an unfavourable judgment from the noblest philosophers and statesmen of the Roman world. For they could only judge the system by its doctrine; and they felt no hesitation in rejecting, as the enemy of the human race, a provisional religion which considered per-

---

* Comte, Catechism of Positive Religion, p. 10.

fection as consisting in an entire concentration upon heavenly objects."* It was the admirable priesthood of Catholicism which modified and interpreted a scheme which, though resting upon such unsafe foundations, contained many important elements which might be, and actually were, made the basis of a grand and powerful organisation. We can form some notion of the debt which Europe owes to Catholicism when we contrast the activity and exuberance of religious thought in the Church itself and also in the schismatic churches which have sprung from it, with its impoverished state among the stagnant Christian communities of the East. Much of the difference no doubt is due to race, but much also to the noble efforts of a priesthood which directed all its energies to the task of securing a convergence of opinion, upon religious matters, till its social and moral mission was complete, when the pent-up waters of the intellectual torrent might burst with a mitigated fury and diminished chance of danger against the solid bulwarks which had been raised upon the ruins of the Empire of the West. Hence we find that from the first the Catholic Church wisely discouraged the barren and disorganising intellectualism of the Alexandrian theologians, and concentrated all its energies upon the consolidation of the spiritual power and the improvement of the social and moral condition of those entrusted to its pastoral charge.

The great logical strength of Catholicism springs from its *principle of authority*—a principle not transitory and open to ever-renewed discussion, but permanent and infallible. Resting as Christianity does upon a written revelation which admits of different meanings, it necessarily demands an interpreter in whom all can trust, (that is, if any lasting convergence of opinion is to be secured.) Now Catholicism claims to provide such an interpreter, and hence—though not proof against the assaults of traitors from within or of

* Comte, Catechism of Positive Religion, p. 10.

total unbelievers from without—it is secure from the attacks of those incautious foes who pretend to accept its dogmatic basis, but refuse to recognise that sacred bond without which the so-called basis is but an unstable quicksand, which, giving way at length, must bring down the edifice reared upon it with ignominious ruin and confusion. The Protestant position is thus well-indicated by the author of 'Rationalism and Faith.' "Religious knowledge requires a basis, an authority whose utterances *can be brought home without question* to the intellect of each individual it influences. B may believe in A as a teacher sent from God, and invested with divine authority; but if B has no means of knowing what A teaches him, his faith in A in no way advances his religious knowledge. If, in every question which is raised, A's authority can be adduced with similar force for *both* of the contending opinions, and there is no means of determining with certainty which is right and which is wrong in claiming his support, it is self-evident that a society of sects and opinions must be the *necessary* result, for which this state of things—*viz.* the unsatisfactory character of A's teaching—is certainly responsible. But from the eternal warfare of sects, and opinions jarring against one another, owing to the adoption of this very principle of individual interpretation of what A said, without allowing A any opportunity of deciding between their interpretations, religious indifference is the natural and certain fruit; men find that they cannot decide between rival tenets; that a learned work can be written on one side, and a similarly learned reply on the other; and consequently, (and not unreasonably from their premises,) infer that neither can be established to the reasonable satisfaction of a learned, still less of an unlearned man." The Catholic doctrine on the other hand, is "that Christ, when He ascended into heaven, left behind him a Church in which the third person of the Blessed Trinity perpetually dwells, for the purpose of teaching all truth, so that whatever the Church teaches is the teaching not of men only, but of God." This theory is certainly an extremely neat one, and if we only grant that Christ *did* ascend into heaven (an important concession of course and not to be made without due deliberation,) we do not see how it is to be controverted : for Christ, who came to save that which was lost, would surely not have augmented the already large catalogue of perdition by leaving to his followers an inheritance of confusion and doubt, by inducing them to embark on a vessel, launched amid the stormy waters of speculation, without a star to enlighten the darkness, or a compass to direct its course.

We are by no means disposed to agree with the author of 'Rationalism and Faith' when he maintains that Christianity and Science are only *apparently* hostile. To our mind the complete triumph of Science is quite incompatible with the existence of *any* Theology. The methods of Science and Theology are radically opposed, the former bringing all phenomena under the control of invariable laws, the latter, even when it admits the cosmic hypothesis most fully, always keeping in reserve a possible arbitrary element in the Divine Will, which may interfere at any moment to upset the stable equilibrium which reigns in the universe of Law. But this is a large question and branches off in so many directions, that it would be quite impossible for us to do justice to it here.

The discussion on *faith* is interesting and well worked out; though we are not ourselves convinced by it. We admit that our notions of right and wrong are instinctive, but we can see no reason why in the practice they should not be made to cluster round an idealised Humanity as well as round a Being to whom we are united simply by the bond of a creation which He must have indulged in for His own satisfaction, and certainly not for the benefit of mankind in general if it be true, as Christianity assures us, that "many are called but few are chosen."

Various are the important topics suggested by this excellent little pamphlet, to which we only wish that we could have done more ample justice. In conclusion we can strongly recommend to our readers the perusal of 'Rationalism and Faith' as a bracing intellectual exercise, and as a valuable specimen of controversy carried on in a fair and tolerant spirit. However much we may differ from the author in his conclusions, we cannot but confess that these conclusions have been arrived at after long and mature thought, while they are upheld in spirit which, if it were the necessary growth of Catholicism, would induce us to regret that we too were not of the fold of St. Peter.

———ooo———

2.—THE *FORTNIGHTLY* ON UTILITARIANISM.

There appeared, a few months ago, in the *Fortnightly Review*, an article upon Mr. Lecky's recent work, "The History of European Morals." The sole object of this article, apparently, is to point out what the writer considers to be certain mistakes into which Mr. Lecky has fallen in his interpretation of the doctrines of Utilitarianism. The writer, however, is not content with simply criticising Mr. Lecky; he, moreover, thinks it is necessary to indulge occasionally in the most flippant and uncalled-for abuse. Every page of the article is replete with passages conceived in the worst taste: the Editor of the *Fortnightly* has evidently forgotten that he is dealing with an adversary who, whatever his demerits may be, always writes like a scholar and a gentleman. As it would be only wasting the time of our readers to point out in detail the passages to which we allude, we shall at once pass on to more important considerations.

The *modern* school of Utilitarians endeavour, it would seem,* to build up a wall of separation between the *test* and the *source* of Morality. Sometimes it is contended that Utilitarianism deals only with the *test*, and has nothing whatever to do with the *source* of morality: if so, Utilitarianism is, by the confession of its own advocates, convicted of a manifest deficiency, since it affords no solution of the most important and most difficult half of the great moral problem. But let us ask,—On what grounds are Utilitarians, of every shade, at war with the so-called Intuitional School? The Intuitionist† says that there is in man an inherent tendency to Virtue, an innate capacity for distinguishing between right and wrong. The Utilitarian denies this. Now, in denying it, does he not by implication assert that he has a theory of his own as to the *source* of morality, and does not all the world know tolerably well what the essential nature of that theory, in the majority of cases, will be? When a man avows himself to be a Utilitarian, can it not, as a rule, be predicted that he will regard Conscience as a compound faculty—derived partly from external circumstances, and partly from internal elements which are wholly unethical? And if men in general can be converted to such a belief, do Utilitarians expect that it will have no influence upon the practice of morality? If so, they can have but a very feeble appreciation of the manner in which all our beliefs are intertwined, and of the mutual actions and reactions which take place between them.

Again the Utilitarian vocabulary is misleading, the terms in which the elementary propositions are couched being often repugnant to the moral consciousness of

---

* We are obliged to employ some such qualification because it is impossible to pin down modern Utilitarians as a class to any definite body of ethical doctrines.

† We employ this term as one in general use, but we do not accept it as describing accurately our own position. Comte's Theory of morals is the one we adopt.

ordinary men. Great use is made of such words as *utility, pleasure, happiness,* &c which, according to the popular usage, have no strictly ethical connotation: the result is, that each proposition requires an elaborate explanation, so that the tyro in ethical studies is often startled at the discrepancy which he observes between the repulsive enunciation of a Utilitarian theorem, and the wholesome conclusions which are deduced from a special interpretation of it. A system which thus, at first sight, shocks the empirical morality of mankind, must certainly contain elements which ought either to be modified or abandoned. The Utilitarian, when thus attacked, defends himself by saying that common language "is only the exponent of current notions and unanalysed impressions of sense," and that the old phrases often require modification. Now this defence, it appears to us, embodies a thorough misconception of the nature and importance of *language*; and, moreover, is untenable because the utilitarian does more than *modify* the old phrases, he utterly changes their meaning, uproots them, as it were, from their old resting places in the moral consciousness of Humanity. The biblical illustration,—(namely, the miracle of Joshua in the valley of Ajalon)—which the Editor of the *Fortnightly* employs in order to elucidate his position, is most unfortunate. Astronomy and Morals are both sciences it is true, but the phenomena with which they respectively deal belong to two widely different categories. The lower any subject is in the scale of human conceptions the fewer are the correct empirical data with which man starts, but the easier is the elaboration of the corresponding science; the higher the subject is, the greater is the body of well-defined, easily-acquired empirical truths with which we commence, but, at the same time, the more difficult is the process by which the subject itself is placed upon a strictly scientific basis. Now Astronomy being one of the least complex and therefore lowest subjects, there were, at the commencement, but few empirical data available for scientific purposes—hence men's astronomical conceptions were necessarily crude and inaccurate, from a strictly scientific point of view. But not so with Morals: for here we find that, from the very dawn of history, men were in possession of a large body of empirical truths which have never since been essentially modified, although Morals, as a science, has not till quite recently been placed upon a really scientific basis.* The empirical moral results attained by the earliest investigators are recorded in every language. There is no civilised language, certainly, (no barbarous one, we believe,) which has not an ethical nomenclature, and in every language this nomenclature is grounded upon the same results. Our Utilitarian system-makers seem to forget that each language is in itself a philosophy, that it records in brief the toilsome investigations, the hardly-won conclusions of the noblest and most intelligent servants of Humanity in the past, and that it has so fixed the *prejudices* (if they may be thus termed) of morality in the minds of men, that it is utterly chimerical, at the present day, to attempt to uproot them. To us then it seems, (whether we consider the matter from a theoretical or from a practical point of view,) that language, so far as it embodies the fundamental moral conceptions of mankind, requires no modification—these conceptions, from the very nature of the case, being unsusceptible of change.†

The attempt made by *some*, if not by all, Utilitarians to resolve conscience into certain elements—none of which are directly ethical—appears to us idle as well as mischievous. We doubt if any really satisfactory

* We believe that it has been so placed by the labours of Gall and Comte. Even those who differ from us may still, many of them, accept the above general statement.

† We do not mean by this that morality, as a whole, cannot advance; but merely that there are a large number of moral ideas definitely fixed from the commencement.

analysis ever has or ever can be given. In any case, the labour wasted upon such tasks might be spent much more usefully in other directions—in strengthening the biological basis of morality, for example. Can it add either to our *knowledge* or to our *virtue* to learn that the conditions required for the production of conscience are such as follow?—(1) The innate susceptibiliy to pain and pleasure. (2) The institution of some external authority, which imposes rules and enforces them by rewards and punishments. (3) The law of contiguous association. Even admitting that it were impossible to prove logically that the reasoning employed to sustain such a thesis was incorrect, we should still renounce the conclusions, because they are useless for all practical purposes, and we feel certain that the moral instincts of men in general* (which are not to be violated with impunity) would rebel against them. There are many things which can be *proved* but which are utterly useless for any good end; we regard this conscience-problem as one of them. After such a confession of our faith, we are quite prepared to have vials of wrath poured upon us by all those who would make *intellect* the supreme dictator in the cerebral commonwealth. Our fundamental maxim is,—" Act from affection, and think in order to act"— in other words, Let all our reasoning have some practical end in view, and let the intellect be ever controlled by moral considerations. In accordance with this maxim we should put aside as utterly useless all the ingenious puzzles of the Utilitarian psychology.

The Editor of the *Fortnightly* more than once accuses Mr. Lecky of making cool statements with tranquil unconsciousness. Now it seemed to us that, as

---

* As against the Positivist, it may be said that with such views the belief in the existence of a First Cause ought to be accepted. The only answer is, that there is a general tendency in the present day to substitute a human basis for a supernatural one. There is no indication of any change in the fundamental moral instincts.

coming from one so very sensitive upon such points, the following statement was, to say the least, startling :—" With the *partial** exception of Bentham no inductive moralist of repute ever omitted to recognise the existence of a moral faculty, or consciousness of obligation." So then Bentham the great founder of *modern* Utilitarianism is to be disposed of as a mere *partial* exception. He is but one in point of quantity, it is true, but in point of quality such a one that we should be inclined to regard him as an exception of very peculiar importance. We had always imagined that Bentham was the head of a large and important school, the members of which entertained an unbounded admiration for *all* the characteristic doctrines of their great master.

"Mr. Mill" says the Editor, "has shown that those who deny the sense of obligation to be simple and innate, are not precluded from calling the obligation natural, for, even if acquired, it has a natural basis in the social affections." From this we should suppose that Mr. Mill, at least, regards the social affections as ultimate elements in the constitution of man. But if the Utilitarian grants the inherence and spontaneity of the social affections, he really grants the whole point in dispute between himself and his adversaries. For these affections are at once the source and the criterion of all morality ; from them emanates the first protest against our personal and selfish instincts, and by their growth the progress of man, from a barbarous to a civilised state, is chiefly characterised. "The source of real morality" says Comte, " lies in the direct exercise of our social sympathies whether systematic or spontaneous." To constitute a science of moral chemistry, which shall enable us to decompose our most important

---

* The italics are ours.—It would be satisfactory to know for certain whether the new school accepts Bentham or not. Apparently it is quite a hopeless task to discover the origin of this school. While their antecedents are so obscure, how can they expect to be thoroughly understood or rightly appreciated ?

moral conceptions into certain non-ethical mental elements fused and transformed by the action of external stimuli—is a lamentable waste of ingenuity, and is calculated to have the most disastrous effect upon our moral spontaneity, if the attempt could, by any possibility, be successful.

Knowing what we do of the doctrines of Paley, Bentham, and James Mill, can the following sentence be regarded as altogether worthy of so exacting a critic as the Editor of the *Fortnightly* ?—"He (Hume) pronounced utility to be the criterion of all virtue; and it has *usually* been supposed that this doctrine *constitutes utilitarianism**." Now can it be maintained, with any degree of candour, that Utilitarianism implies no more than a certain criterion of morality? It has been already pointed out that the hostility which subsists between the Utilitarian school and the Intuitionists, involves at least the profession of some peculiar opinions as to the source of morality, and that these opinions must, to a certain extent, react both upon the theory and upon the practice of morality. It is not denied by Utilitarians themselves that there may be some among them who regard utility as at once the *source* and the *test* of right and wrong, but it is assumed that such opinions go for nothing, and that, as all are agreed upon the test, opponents have no right to break through and disturb this delightful unanimity. Whether the out-and-out advocates of utility are such a contemptible minority as to justify Mr. J. S. Mill and his school in arrogating to themselves the title of Utilitarians *par excellence*, we should think is open to grave doubt :—it is possible that if the Editor of the *Fortnightly* were to classify all the great ethicists who have advocated this doctrine under some form or other, from Epicurus downwards, he would find it necessary to furnish his readers with another instance of *partial* exceptions.

* The italics are ours.

But if Utilitarians have indeed come to the conclusion that the sum and substance of their system is that virtue always benefits mankind; then let them *coram populo* lay aside whatever else has *usually* been mixed up with the notion of Utility. Let them also adopt the suggestion of the Editor of the *Fortnightly* and call themselves the Beneficentials, for while they persist in retaining the name of Utilitarians they mislead their fellow-men, and cannot justly complain if they are misunderstood. It is simply absurd to suppose that all who have criticised the doctrine of utility, and have drawn from it unfavourable conclusions, have been pursuing a chimæra, a phantom of their own brains. If the doctrine is so easily misunderstood, what guarantee is there that simple men, who may chance to apply it in every-day life, will not fall into the same, or even worse errors than the historians and philosophers who have considered, criticised, and mistaken it? Is the Utilitarian arithmetic of such a nature that a Cleon is likely to prove himself a more skilful accountant than a Pericles or a Plato?*

The arbitrary manner in which these recent interpreters of the old Cyrenaic dogma† deal with some of its most celebrated advocates, is well exhibited in the following sentence :—"It is true that in a writer like Mandeville, and in a much less degree in Paley, this theory of the standard of morals has been presented in phrases and with a spirit which invest it with an air of very marked coarseness and meanness." From such language as this, and from a remark which occurs shortly after about the "eccentricities of early teachers," one would suppose that Mr. Lecky was bound

---

* No doubt it will be objected to this, that Utilitarian theorists do not intend that such calculations should be generally undertaken; yet surely the statements made by certain members of this school do imply that the discovery of *right* (even in the case of individual morality) involves a process of calculation. Utilitarianism talks largely about amounts of happiness, but does it anywhere propose a definite human ideal for our imitation?

† Pleasure constitutes the highest happiness, and must consequently be the end of all human exertions.

to furnish his readers with an exposition of modern Epicureanism as it is mirrored in the mind of the Editor of the Fortnightly, and not as it is found in the works of those accomplished writers and eminent thinkers, in the past, who have shed a lustre upon the literatures of their respective countries, and have enriched the history of Philosophy with imperishable monuments. But Mr. Lecky, from the very nature of his subject, was not concerned with Utilitarianism in its most recent form. His object was to explain the causes which have led to the present low moral ideal which obtains among large classes of European society: for this purpose, it was not necessary that he should notice, even indirectly,* Utilitarianism in "its best and most developed stage." This sublime form of Epicureanism may perchance have a great influence upon the morals of the 20th century, but it has produced as yet only a very limited and scarcely appreciable effect upon the general mass of European society. Because Mr. Lecky is sometimes inaccurate, and fails to appreciate properly the most advanced form of a certain doctrine, we cannot see that he has rendered himself amenable to the strong imputations of unfairness brought against him by the Editor of the Fortnightly.† Mr. Lecky is the last man in the world whom we should accuse of bigotry or dishonesty. He always, at least, endeavours to be fair, and if at times he may inadvertently do injustice to a doctrine or to an individual, his opponent is not, on that account, entitled to insinuate that Mr. Lecky systematically adopts " the pious habit or duty of misrepresenting an adversary." Such language is neither courteous nor just.

---

* He has noticed it, we are aware; and we are willing to allow that he has misjudged it. It would have been better if he had completely ignored it.

† The allusion made by the Editor to the unfairness of the Christian clergy is worse than the very worst of Mr. Lecky's delinquencies; and quite unworthy, we should have thought, of a professor of the sublime Utilitarian gospel.

It has often been urged that the calculations required by the Utilitarian ethics could not be performed by ordinary men. No calculations, however, appear to be too complicated for the great masters of the faith. The task to be performed is thus naively described by the Editor :—"He (the Utilitarian philosopher) takes all the phenomena connected with the distinction between right and wrong; examines them, analyses them, considers them in connection with the general laws of the mental operations of mankind, and finally arrives at a certain idea of the one principle, quality, law or essential condition, that regulates the distinction about which he has been busy." Where the records of these complicated operations are to be found we have yet to learn. The rare ingenuity of Bentham, as displayed in his elaborate ethical tables, must sink into insignificance when compared with that of our model Utilitarian who "seeks the standard of morality by the light of consciousness, of course, in a sense, but in the other facts of human experience." After the accomplishment of the laborious task above indicated, it is discovered (1) That the invariable condition of right is, that it conduces to the happiness of the human community, and (2) That actions are virtuous because they, directly or indirectly, are conducive to happiness. So much analysis, arrangement, and classification appear to be quite unnecessary in order to arrive at the first conclusion ; and it must be highly annoying, after the expense of much valuable energy, to find that the second conclusion is indignantly repudiated by the *simple consciousness* of mankind. Considering the herculean labours which these "methodical and reason-following investigators of experience" are obliged to undergo, Mr. Lecky must be hard-hearted indeed if he does not, in some measure, sympathise with his adversary, when that adversary indignantly exclaims, "What sort of scientific spirit can a writer have who supposes that he is overturning conclusions *thus gained*, by merely confronting them with the simply followed consciousness of mankind ?" But is this simple consciousness of mankind really so value-less a guide as the Editor of the Fortnightly would have us believe ? Even in Religion and Astronomy (which are the subjects he has chosen for the illustration of his views) are its conclusions to be utterly rejected ? Do we not, even in such subjects as these, still attach a value and a meaning to the fundamental primitive conceptions ? Does not the poet still animate the external world with feeling and activity ? Is the process of abstraction, typified in history by the advance from Fetichism to Polytheism, yet extinct ? And finally that great primeval heresy, which makes sun, moon and stars but greater or lesser lights appointed to circulate about the earth, does not even it hold good, in a certain sense, to the scientific as well as to the popular mind ?—But even admitting, as we willingly do, that in the lower sciences there are but few of the primitive conceptions which do not require considerable modification, still, as we have before remarked, these conceptions become more and more trustworthy the higher we ascend the scale of human knowledge. The unaided experience of man could advance but a little way in such sciences as Astronomy or Chemisty, it could advance somewhat further in Physiology, and a very long way indeed in Morals. Hence although we should distrust the dicta of simple consciousness in Chemistry and Physiology, (which are the sciences adduced in the challenge of the Fortnightly,) we should be inclined to give great weight to these dicta when testing the results of any particular theory of Morals. There are certain writers who appear to think that a theory best fulfils its end when it succeeds in completely upsetting the ordinary notions of ordinary men ; whereas, all science, as Comte observes, is but the prolongation and systematisation of sound common sense.

It will be observed that, in the two conclusions arrived at by the Utilitarian mode of procedure, nothing is said *directly* about the *agent*. We are merely told (1) that the invariable condition of right is conducing to the happiness of the community, and (2) that an action is virtuous because it promotes happiness. And this brings us to another of the characteristic doctrines of the school, namely, the separation between *actions* and *agents*—which is, in fact, but another form of the separation between the *test* and the *source* of morality (a tenet to which we have before alluded.) It is alleged that the act done can be considered by the moralist without any reference to the agent doing it; and it is supposed that the results arrived at, after this process of elimination, will be highly valuable. To test the doctrine, let us select any miscellaneous group of actions, and proceed to classify them—guided only by the naked principle,—*Actions are virtuous which produce happiness.* How, in this case are we to avoid registering among virtuous actions such performances as—constructing machines, ploughing fields, and cutting canals? Yet Mr. Lecky is overwhelmed with a torrent of indignant and vehement logic, because he has pointed out this very obvious difficulty, though from a somewhat different point of view. In spite of the imposing shade of Aldrich which has been evoked on this occasion, and the playful irony of Socrates which has also been called in to the aid of the courteous champion of Utilitarianism, we fail to perceive the untrustworthiness of Mr. Lecky's conclusion. The historian of European morals is not the first who has pointed out this serious objection to the doctrine of utility. Greater men than Mr. Lecky (it may be said without offence) have discerned and explained the radical incompatibility that exists between our conceptions of *virtue* and *utility*. But our modern utilitarians seem to regard the history of philosophy in the same light that they regard the language of ordinary men—as something wholly delusive, and requiring to be completely remodelled. Adam Smith, for example, was not a writer likely to be deceived by a transparent sophism, yet he distinctly says, "it seems impossible that the approbation of virtue should be a sentiment of the same kind with that by which we approve of a convenient and well-contrived building; or that we should have no other reason for praising a man than that for which we commend a chest of drawers.*" And yet, with this and many similar criticisms of other great moralists staring us in the face, we are summoned in a tone of authority to believe that it is very meet, right and our bounden duty to accept utility as a safe index in our search for virtuous actions.† But it would appear, upon the showing of the Editor himself, that the mere classification of actions as virtuous, or otherwise, is not sufficient, because when we have determined what actions are virtuous, it still remains to be discovered what particular degree of virtue each action possesses; so that a rule is required to determine the rank of each in the ethical scale. What is this rule? If rank also is to be determined by the amount of happiness conferred, we submit that this principle is too vague to be of any practical service, and that the previous difficulty would still occur under another form;—For if we refuse to take the agent into account, we can, if we are consistent, regard various sorts of happiness as differing only in *strength* and not in *kind*.‡ In classifying

---

* It is quite possible that Utilitarians will endeavour to evade this objection by having recourse to their favourite dogma of the separation between actions and agents. To us, however, it seems that such a separation rather enhances the difficulty than otherwise.

† Bentham, the great forerunner of Mill and his school, thus defines the principle of utility:—"That principle which approves or disapproves of every action whatever, according to the tendency which it appears to have to augment or diminish the happiness of the *party whose interest is in question*." And yet with such a definition as this before us, we are told that utilitarianism is essentially unselfish and humane (in the largest sense of the term.)

‡ Paley consistently defines *happiness* as "a certain state of the nervous system in that part of the human frame in which we feel joy and grief, passions and affections." We do not agree with Paley, but he is thoroughly pellucid, as clear and fearless a thinker, in his way, as Comte.

actions according to the happiness they produce, without reference to the moral conceptions of the agent, we may determine with tolerable accuracy the category of *wrong*; but we can never, on such a principle, avoid mixing up with what is *right* that which is morally *indifferent*. Hence the Utilitarian classification, even if it could be successfully framed, would be of little use to the moralist who has to determine what is right, though it might be of some service to the legislator whose chief business is to decide what is hurtful and wrong. Mr. Lecky says "A feeling of satisfaction follows the accomplishment of duty for itself, but if the duty be performed solely through the expectation of the mental pleasure, conscience refuses to ratify the bargain." In commenting upon this the Editor of the *Fortnightly* remarks, that it is *to this feeling of satisfaction that the utilitarian moralist appeals.*—In so doing, we think he errs. It was to no such feeling that Chivalry of old appealed. *Fais ce que dois, advienne que pourra** was the principle acted on by the medieval knight,—a principle, it appears to us, considerably in advance of the modern Utilitarian one, though we are prepared to hear from some of our teachers that it is both vague and impracticable, or from others that it concerns only the agent and not the act. As this question of Duty is just one of those upon which Positivism brings its doctrine of Humanity to bear in the most admirable manner, it may not be out of place here to explain the Positivist Theory of Duty. In Positivism, Duty is regarded as the bond which connects the individual or the community with Humanity—past, present, and future. From Humanity, in the past and present, each one of us has received all that he possesses, and to the service of Humanity, therefore, each one is bound to consecrate all his energies—moral, intellectual, and physical. The feeling of satisfaction (in the

---

* Do thy duty, come what may.

individual,) which follows the accomplishment of duty is but a secondary consideration, and should be kept, as far as possible, in the background. It is gratitude for the manifold blessings conferred upon the individual by Humanity, in the past and the present, to which alone the Positivist moralist directs his appeal.*

There is, in the present day, a considerable class of thinkers who have, some in a greater some in a less degree, imbibed the doctrines of Comte, and who yet refuse to recognise the debt which they owe to him : they calmly appropriate some of his most characteristic opinions and publish them, in treatises intended for the general reader, as if they were original discoveries.† It would be unjust to rank Mill in this category, since he has always borne a willing testimony to the vast influence which Comte has exercised upon the whole sphere of modern thought : but it would be well if he were to discourage his English admirers when they ascribe to his initiative the working-out of conceptions for which we really are indebted to the pressure of Positivism. It is to Comte we feel certain that all the recent developments of practical morality,‡ (so far as they are not spontaneous) are due, and it is mainly the influence of his teaching which has brought about the downfal of the old Utili-

---

* In Positivism our *instincts of benevolence* are regarded as the common source both of Duty and of happiness. Comte says, " None but the sympathetic instincts can have free scope without any check, for in giving these play each individual is aided by all the others, whereas his personal instincts, on the contrary, find a constant check from others. In this way it will appear that happiness and duty must necessarily coincide."

† We regard Mr. Lecky as one of those who have not been just to Comte. Mr. Lecky's doctrine that there is in man a spontaneous tendency to good from which, as from a primitive germ, the highest morality has been very gradually developed—is essentially Comtian. Again Mr. Lecky's account of the Middle Ages affords an admirable illustration of Comte's views regarding the part played by Catholicism in the education of the West; and yet, strange to say, Mr. Lecky speaks in the most disparaging terms of the Positivist theory of Mediævalism.

‡ Such, for instance, as the application of moral considerations in all *industrial* and *international* questions.

tarian school, represented in England by such thinkers as Paley and Bentham. As for the Neo-Utilitarianism of the present day, so far as it has any value at all, it is but a mutilated form of one half of Comte's moral system, which, as all readers of the *Catechism* or *Politique* will remember, consists of two parts, one scientific and the other chiefly practical: it is the latter of these in which we find all the really valuable principles enunciated by the new school of Utilitarian moralists.* Now as the Editor of the Fortnightly is manifestly acquainted with the labours of Comte, and is moreover an ardent admirer of certain noble qualities the absence of which he deplores in Mr. Lecky, what interpretation are we to put upon the following remarkable statement?—"The development of the utilitarian or *beneficential*† ethics is more and more evidently the next advance in moral philosophy. Of this development Mr. Mill's treatise marked the *true beginning*." So all that Comte has done in *beneficential* Morality, years before Mr. Mill published his treatise, is to go for nothing. The great philosopher who organised the doctrine of Humanity, who formulated the noble precept *Live for others*, who in season and out of season proclaimed the exquisite charm and manifest dignity of our social sympathies,—made no *true beginning*, his labours are to be utterly ignored, his name not even mentioned in terms of passing commendation. All the honours of the future victories which Sociability is destined to gain in its contest with Selfishness, are to be reserved for the great captain-general of the bene-

---

* There is no doubt that several of this school are acquainted with Comte, and yet they never even mention his name in connection with morals.

† Comte has introduced the term *altruistic* to denote the social, unselfish part of man's nature. The term is neat and expressive, and in every way preferable to beneficential. But English writers will always persist in improving upon the good which the gods provide them.

Perhaps we ought to state here that a Utilitarian would consider the terms *altruistic* and *beneficential* to be wide as the poles asunder; because, as he would inform us, the one relates to agents, and the other to actions. We regard the constant employment of this distinction as altogether mischievous; it affords a loophole for the most pitiful moral sophistry.

ficential forces Mr. J. S. Mill, and for such lieutenants as the Editor of the Fortnightly.

Finally we are told that " utilitarianism either in its grosser form, or, with better minds, in its form as a highly rationalised kind of Christianity, may be described as practically the dominant creed of the time.*" We presume that the Editor of the Fortnightly is to be classed among the *better minds* who adopt the creed in its highly rationalised kind of Christian form (whatever that may mean.) But what is Utilitarianism in its grosser form? Is it such as Mr. Lecky has described it? Because if so, we fail to see how that distinguished writer is amenable to the terrible censures of the *highly rationalised Christian* Utilitarian. The problem which Mr. Lecky has attempted to solve is precisely this—To trace the effects of Utilitarianism in its grosser form, upon the general tone of society in modern Europe. And yet the chief objection urged against the substance of his reasoning is, that he has libelled Utilitarianism in taking the grosser form as the typical one. We were surprised indeed after wading through several pages of the Fortnightly's scornful rhetoric to discover that Utilitarianism did still exist in its grosser form. Surely, if this is admitted, it would be more becoming on the part of the new Utilitarian school to withhold their terrible anathemas against the errors of such as have not been initiated into all the mysteries of their faith, until some name has been discovered which may enable the outer world to distinguish the highly rationalised Christians from their grosser associates.

---

* In ludicrous contrast with the patronising tone here adopted towards Christianity, is the language of a passage (occurring in the same number of the Fortnightly, and only two pages further on,) in which Mr. A. C. Swinburne is allowed to describe the religion of Dante and of Milton as "the most hateful creed in all history; uglier than the faith of Moloch or of Kali, by the hideous monsuetude, the devilish loving-kindness of its elections and damnations." Mr. Swinburne ranks Homer, Æschylus, Sophocles, and Shakespeare, above both Dante and Milton, because they are (as he expresses it, in his usual fervid, alliterative style) "clean from the pollution of this pestilence" (meaning Christianity.) Hence it is probable that to this last-born of the "sons of light" the neo-utilitarian creed will seem no better than a highly rationalised kind of pestilence.

Every thing in connection with this new-fashioned Utilitarianism is vague except its so called beneficential or altruistic principle, which is worked out far better in Positivism. What definite idea is to be formed of the belief of one who calls himself a highly rationalised kind of Christian, we are at a loss to discover.* It seems to us much the same as if a Christian convert, in ancient times, had described himself to an idolatrous public as a highly rationalised kind of Polytheist. St. Paul tells us that he was all things to all men; but we have yet to learn that he presented himself to the Jews as a highly rationalised kind of Pharisee, or to the Greeks as a highly rationalised kind of worshipper of the gods of Olympus. If beneficential Utilitarians are indeed anxious to found a new Religion let them adopt a definite and intelligible name, organise a complete body of doctrine, frame a *cultus*, and furnish a *regime* of life. The world will understand them then, and they will have all lovers of consistency and straight-forwardness on their side—their followers will know exactly what they are required to believe, and their adversaries will no longer combat with a foe which, like some oiled wrestler in the palæstra, continually slips from beneath their grasp. For Utilitarian free-thinkers to connect themselves in any way with Christianity, is an artifice which will conciliate neither Christians nor the great bulk of those who have practically abandoned Christianity. They may depend upon it that the frank hostility of the Positivist will be more welcome in the long run to the sincere Christian, than the insidious friendship of those, who like the Mahratta chieftain, proffer false embraces, wearing a panoply of war concealed beneath the outer garb of peace. As for the non-Christian part of the

---

* Perhaps this designation has been constructed on the eclectic principle and indicates that the Neo-utilitarian creed is a combination of Ultrarationalism, Christianity, and Epicureanism. In accordance with this hypothesis each true believer would be a Strauss, a Wilberforce, and a Bentham, gathered into one.

community it can matter little to them by what name
men call themselves so long as they are honest and
their doctrines are intelligible : in canvassing for the
suffrages of this large and increasing class we feel
sure that those who loyally acknowledge their creed
and master, condescending to no subterfuges, will eventually be preferred to those who come before their fel-
low-citizens with a transparent falsehood inscribed
upon their banners.

———ooo———

3.—THE RELIGIOUS TENDENCIES OF INDIA.

THERE appeared in the last October number of the
Dublin Quarterly Review an able article on "The
Religious Tendencies of India." The writer is evidently well acquainted with the subject of which he
treats ; and, whatever we may think of his conclusions, it cannot be denied that he has expressed his
views temperately and clearly, and that he has always
spoken with respect even of opinions to which he is
most thoroughly opposed. But as he is at once both a
sincere and intelligent Catholic, it is only natural that
he should point out as forcibly as possible what he
considers to be the fundamental errors of non-Catho-
lics, and that he should warmly advocate the claims
of Catholicism to universal acceptance.

The object of the article, as expressed by the writer
himself, is " to invite attention to the relation between
Catholicity and the phases of religious speculation
which are now to be found in restless activity in all
parts of India that have been most permeated with
Western civilization and education."

After taking a brief survey of the antecedents and
present circumstances of Catholic missions in India,
some interesting remarks are made upon the intellectual and religious position of the non-Aryan (or, as we
should prefer to call them, Fetichistic) races. The Reviewer alludes to the successes which the Lutheran
missionaries have gained in dealing with these races,

and suggests that they afford a fair and promising field for future Catholic enterprise. The reasons given for the rapid spread of Protestantism among these rude aboriginal tribes, seem to us wholly inadequate. The secret of such successes arises from the circumstance that Fetichism has no organised creed, and therefore presents very little resistance to the invasion of a foreign religion,* so long as that religion is content to accommodate itself, in some degree, to the feelings and prejudices of a simple-minded, unreflecting, impulsive people. Wherever there is a highly organised religious creed, Christianity fails to make conversions on any large scale. Hence it is absolutely powerless when brought face to face with Mahometanism, and among Hindoos its influence is confined, almost exclusively, to the very lowest classes where the mental development has not advanced much beyond the primitive stage. The Reviewer, however, appears to be fully conscious that a system of proselytism which may succeed well enough among Coles and Sonthals cannot be applied without considerable modifications to Hindoos.

In considering the influence of Christianity upon Hindooism, the Reviewer commences with an estimate of the obstacles presented by the complicated social environment to the introduction of a new and revolutionary creed. His remarks upon the conservative influence of caste prove him to be one who is endowed with wide sympathies as well as with an acute understanding. He says, " at the very outset of missionary enterprise, the progress of Christianity among the lower castes only, tended to augment tenfold the repugnance and hostility of the Brahmins and other high-caste Hindoos. It cannot be too often insisted on, that caste is a social as well as a religious distinction ; Christianity thus not only appeared in the eyes

---

* Even in China, where Fetichism is most developed, we find Buddhism Mahometanism, and Catholicism effecting an easy entrance.

of Hindoos as a religious innovation, but as the creed
of socialism and license, which allied itself with all
that was lowest and most infamous in the country.
In propagating opinions of any kind, it is always ha-
zardous to ignore the natural leaders of a community,
and attempt to win over the multitude without their
co-operation." These remarks we most cordially en-
dorse; they exhibit, we think, a thoroughly just appreciation of the course to be pursued in all important
social or religious movements. They are especially
valuable at a time like the present when the friends of
innovation are loudly advocating the adoption of a
wide system of secular education for the masses of
India, without carefully reflecting upon the consequences that may ensue from unsettling the beliefs and prejudices of the multitude at so early a stage of the
national development. Let the elite, and none but
the elite, of the Hindoo community be first thoroughly initiated into the civilisation of the West, this task
accomplished, (and it is far from being accomplished
as yet,) it will then be time to consider how the general body of the people may be released from the
restrictions of a religion which has rendered noble
services in the past, but which no longer satisfies the
highest aspirations of the national mind. Hindooism
has, in our opinion, no cause to fear the open and honest warfare waged by Christianity, whether Catholic or Protestant; but there is a foe at its gates
more dangerous than any that it has yet encoun-
tered, a foe whose approaches are insidious and
whose onslaught is deadly, a foe which, like the
angel in the camp of the sleeping Assyrians, smites
its unsuspecting victims without warning and without
remorse. That foe is Scepticism*—it respects no
time-honoured beliefs or institutions, it rejoices in

* We should prefer to designate it Negativism; but as this term is not
frequently used we have adopted one which will be generally understood, although it does not convey all that we wish to imply.

disorder, it destroys without attempting to rebuild; under its corroding influences the foundations of Hindoo society are being gradually undermined at a time when there is absolutely nothing to replace the old organisation. We are nowadays constantly hearing the voice of a crude and empirical rationalism raised in order to decry the magnificent social monuments raised in ancient times by Brahmin theocrats and legislators; and as in the East so in the West, everywhere the past is vilified in order to glorify the present, and the shallow glories of an immature, industrial civilisation are sung with praises never accorded to the greatest triumphs of Humanity in the past. It is chiefly because the doctrines of the revolutionary school thus lead men to regard themselves as supremely wise in their own conceit, that they are so fatal to the community. Such doctrines exercise a most powerful fascination over the minds of the young, and are readily welcomed since they demand no important sacrifice as the price of their acceptance.

But to return to the article under consideration. In order to place in a clear light the obstacles presented by caste to the spread of Christianity, and show what kind of missionaries are required in India, the Reviewer dwells at some length upon the labours of the celebrated Father De Nobili. Tradition tells of the existence of small communities of native Christians in southern India* from very early times. The first introduction of Christianity into the peninsula is

---

* The reason why Christianity has flourished most in Southern India is thus explained by the Reviewer. "There is good reason to believe that the lowest of the four great parent castes into which Hindoo Society is divided, the Sudras, was originally composed in great part of the conquered aborigines who consented to remain in the plains and become the subjects of their invaders. The invasion coming from the North, it can readily be surmised, as indeed is confirmed by experience, that the influence of the conquerors or higher castes is far less supreme in the south than in the north of India: and this is one of the main reasons why the extreme south of the peninsula furnishes by far the most successful fields for Protestant as well as Catholic missionary labour."

assigned to S. Thomas, one of the twelve. But it was not till the middle of the 16th century that any very important results were accomplished. It is to the magnificent enthusiasm of S. Francis Xavier, who gained for the cross so many splendid triumphs throughout the East, that Indian Christianity is chiefly indebted for its distinctive characteristics and rapid development. S. Xavier addressed his preaching almost exclusively to the lower orders, he made no systematic attempt to gain over to his side the aristocracy of Hindooism : hence when his powerful initiative was withdrawn, Catholicism ceased to spread. For more than half a century the successors of the indomitable Spaniard, unable to make any further progress, were principally engaged in consolidating his hasty conquests. Not till the beginning of the 17th century did any one appear upon the scene worthy to take up the mantle let fall by S. Xavier, and to smite with it a second time the rebellious waters of Hindoo Polytheism. It was the celebrated Jesuit Robert De Nobili* who first advanced the standards of the cross beyond the limits where his predecessor had fixed them. This remarkable man, well knowing how important it was to secure the co-operation of the upper classes, commenced his labours, after the manner of S. Paul, by becoming a Brahmin to the Brahmins, in order that he might gain the Brahmins.† And here we would observe that the brilliant success attained by the Jesuit missionaries of that age, both in Asia and America, was due, in a great measure, to their wonderful power of sympathy,

---

* Robert De Nobili was a nephew of Cardinal Bellarmine. He established his head quarters at Madura, (a town about 270 miles south of Madras in 1606.

† De Nobili and his colleagues assumed Hindoo names, and introduced themselves as Brahmins of a superior order from the western world. They published works in Sanskrit, on the being and attributes of the Deity, in which the train of argument and phraseology of the sacred Brahminical books were imitated with the most consummate skill.

their rare facility of adaptation to unaccustomed modes of thought and action,—they possessed in an eminent degree the apostolic faculty of being all things to all men, without compromising the fundamental principles of their creed.* The efforts of De Nobili were, at the commencement, attended with marked success; but, the novel method which he employed having aroused considerable opposition among the non-Jesuit orders, his schemes were seriously interfered with, and in consequence of this interference such an unfavourable impression was produced upon the Brahmins that their confidence could never be thoroughly restored. With De Nobili the golden age of evangelisation in India passed away. The systematic attempts made to thwart the efforts of the Jesuit missionaries produced their legitimate results—suspicion and distrust were sown in the minds of the patricians, and Christianity was henceforth obliged to confine itself, as at first, to the proletariate. Brahminism thus escaped the immediate danger which threatened it, and its organisation remained intact for the next two centuries, after the lapse of which period a new and more formidable enemy presented itself under the form of Western Rationalism. It is to a consideration of the revolution which is being gradually accomplished by the unrestricted propagation, during the last half century, of European science and freethought, that the article in the *Dublin Review* is chiefly directed.

The Reviewer, in treating this important subject, begins by describing the twofold action upon the Hindoo mind (1) of Protestant missions, and (2) of the English Government.

(1) *Protestant missions.* As Protestantism is found-

---

* The Jesuits were often censured, even by Catholics, for making too great concessions to unbelievers of every kind. No doubt the dogmas of Christianity are not well adapted for the successful application of Jesuit liberalism.

ed upon negation, it is naturally unadapted to the work of converting those who are not Christians. Undeterred, however, by the inherent difficulties of their position, Protestant missionaries have contended valiantly for the cause entrusted to their charge. When it became manifest that the citadel of Hindooism could not be taken by direct assault, they, nothing daunted, changed their tactics and proceeded to undermine the beleaguered walls. "Having failed," as Mr. Marshall expresses it, "to convert the Hindoo by bibles or preaching, they resolved to try the effect of education." This indirect method of attack found its warmest and most energetic supporters in the missions of the Free Church and Church Missionary Society. "The Hindoos," to employ the Reviewer's words "welcomed the opportunity of learning English, and European sciences, with commendable alacrity. * * * * The prospect of employment, especially under Government, has undoubtedly been the dominant motive which has led Hindoo youths to English schools, aided in a minor degree by a love of knowledge; but these schools have been filled by the children of higher castes, mostly the poorer members of them, who have eagerly accepted the chance, thus afforded them, of redeeming their prospects by employments of that kind which custom and religion have both marked out as their proper sphere. Children of the lower castes have indeed been mixed with them, but in a minority, and, compared with their relative numbers, a vast *proportionate* minority. There may have been occasional reluctance in some instances, as well as alarm, when any actual conversion has taken place, but these are exceptional; the English schools opened by the missionaries have been, as a rule, well filled, and the teachers have been eminently successful in being brought face to face with the *elite* of Hindooism through the medium of the children of the higher classes. That the success of the movement as far as conversions are concerned has been quite out of proportion to its success as an educational movement, is too well known to need repetition : probably not one boy in a hundred who has passed through his course at a missionary school has been converted to Christianity."

(2) *The English Government.* In describing and defending the policy of neutrality pursued by the Government, in matters of religion, the Reviewer makes some admirable observations which we commend to the notice of all who are earnest in the advocacy of political or social reforms. " We are inclined to think" he says " that at the present day the Government is more open to reproach for practically departing from its promises of neutrality and using its power unduly to advance Chistianity, than for repressing or discouraging it. Bishops, Archdeacons, and a considerable staff of Anglican and Presbyterian chaplains are maintained out of revenues almost exclusively, raised from Hindoos and Mahomedans: besides this, liberal rules are enacted for grants in aid of maintaining other clergy, and building or repairing churches wherever they are needed." The large and costly ecclesiastical establishment, maintained by the toiling millions of India for the benefit of a handful of foreigners,* is, in our opinion, a scandal to the civilisation of the 19th century,† a flagrant abuse

---

* The attempts made by Government ecclesiastics to exercise missionary functions only aggravate the evil. All such attempts constitute a direct infringement of the policy of neutrality—they involve too the absurdity of making heathens pay for their own conversion, a process hardly to be defended in an age of such boasted liberality and enlightenment as the present one.

† The great latitudinarian statesmen of the 18th century would never have permitted such an abuse to creep in. It has been allowed to attain its present dimensions, not from any desire to do injustice to the people of India, but simply because there has not been displayed a sufficient strength of will in resisting ecclesiastical encroachments. No doubt the vague religiosity which has been so much in fashion of late years, and on which the present generation plumes itself so highly, has paralysed the efforts of men who would have been willing to pursue a different policy.

which, for the sake of English honour and justice,
ought not to be any longer tolerated. We have
lately seen the Church establishment in Ireland
swept away in obedience to the just demands of
an indignant people, and the unanimous verdict
of British Liberalism. The same arguments which
apply to Ireland may be applied, with even greater
force, to India; and we feel certain that, if the im-
perial legislature should ever give to Indian affairs that
serious attention which they deserve, one of their first
and most obvious measures will be the abolition of an
institution which is as thoroughly useless as it is ano-
malous and unjust.* The Reviewer, in continuance
of his strictures upon the religious policy of the Government, observes,—" Native converts, if not avowed-
ly favoured, enjoy a greater share of official patron-
age than is their due; and the Senate of the Calcutta
University, which is composed of Fellows appointed
exclusively by Government, is filled with Protestant
missionaries and clergy; so much so that on a recent
occasion the missionary element defeated the edu-
cationalists and natives combined in regard to the re-
tention of a particular work, patronised by the missionaries as the exclusive text-book on moral philo-
phy."

Still it must be allowed that the English Government has, in the main, been true to its principles of
religious neutrality. Like the Roman prefects of old,
our administrators have in general been careless about
spiritual matters, and hence their policy has closely
resembled that so admirably described by Gibbon
at the opening of his second Chapter. In considering
the effect of this Gallionism upon state-education, the

* Why could not our financiers, who are so busy in devising schemes
with a view to curtail the national expenditure, turn their attention towards
the unnecesssry burden imposed upon the Indian revenue by the mainte-
nance of a body of ecclesiastics whose spiritual authority is not even recognised by the whole of the dominant race. (1870).

Reviewer incisively remarks—"Many of the governing body over India are and have been deists or sceptics; still more, rationalists and latitudinarians of the most comprehensive type: hence there has been very far from any accord as to the nature of the religious principles, if any, which should be taught, but there has been a very general agreement in the benefits to be anticipated from a wide-spread dissemination of the English language, and of the vast literature to which it forms the key, as well as of all the Western sciences." The Hindoos have shown themselves only too willing to coincide with these views, and hence the Government has been induced to organise an elaborate system of official education which promises completely to revolutionise the national customs and beliefs.

After furnishing his readers with the ordinary statistics, the Reviewer proceeds to explain the effects of the Government educational policy. He says :—

"The results of this wide extension of secular education are perhaps without parallel in the world: crowded as these (Government) schools have been by high-caste Hindoos, the superstitions, prejudices, and religious feelings of the upper classes are being rapidly dissipated. We believe we are not exaggerating in saying that Hindooism, as a religion, is dead : no one who has received an English education believes in it. * * * One of the consequences of this has been to vindicate the conclusions of De Nobili, that caste was still stronger as a social than as a religious institution : many a man who has entirely lost his belief in his religion is zealous and tenacious of his position as a high-caste man, and scrupulously performs all customary rites and ceremonies. He argues as many a better man has argued before him in regard to a religion which has lost its vital hold upon him : 'This is good for the reverential and superstitious feelings of the masses, it is part of a great national and social system intimately

imbedded in the traditions and customs of the people;
if senseless it is harmless, and why should I needlessly
offend even the prejudices of my fellows'?"

Again he observes:—

"Any person who *a priori* considers the probable effect of an
English secular education of the nineteeth century on a Hindoo polytheist and idolater,* will be able to picture with tolerable accuracy
the general character of the result: every thing around him, every
line he reads, every fact he learns, tends to discredit his religious
ideas, and his weak and illogical belief soon totters before attacks which
meet with no resistance from any other quarter. He has lost his
old religion, but has gained nothing in place of it. * * * His reason
is being cultivated all day long, and he gets profoundly well satisfied
with and self-confident in it: he reads of Christianity, it is true,
and he knows well enough that scores of its missionaries are ready
to convert him, but he also learns soon enough that even among
Europeans it has many opponents, and his prejudices being all against
it, he rather reads their works than those of its advocates. Hence
Voltaire, Francis Newman, and Colenso furnish him with an armoury
which enables him entirely to turn the tables upon his missionary
opponents: so far from shunning the controversy, educated natives
often eagerly invite it; they look down upon Christianity as superstitious, ignorant, and behind the age, are confident that it is totter-
ing to its fall, and even believe that they are not unlikely to play
an important part in effecting this result. 'Europe,' they are never
tired of saying, 'has blessed us with the gift of its science and material
civilisation, and we, in return, will repay it by assisting it to root
out its own religious superstitions'."

We are quite willing to allow, (as the Reviewer
here of course implies) that Christianity has little
to fear from the overt hostility of Hindoo sceptics
or deists, but we cannot grant that Hindoo Polytheism
has produced no effect upon the stability and permanence of the Christian religion. It is, in fact,
owing to the wide diffusion and obstinate vitality of
such religions as Hindooism, Buddhism, and Confucian-
ism that Christianity has been unable to make good
its claim to universality; and it is, chiefly, because
there is no prospect that Christianity ever can become

* The term *idolater*, strictly speaking, is only applicable to Fetich-worship-
pers. The Polytheist is not *necessarily* more of an idolater than the
Monotheist.

universal, that men are nowadays looking about for some system which may be the means of eventually uniting all nations, so that it shall become possible to say *everywhere*—There is one body, one spirit, one faith.

Since Hindooism has ceased to be a living power in the minds of those young men who frequent English schools and colleges, and since " the religious instincts of mankind cannot be totally obliterated," it is natural to enquire what is the nature of those religious beliefs which, among Hindoos, survive the wreck of their early faith. On this subject the Reviewer says "A great many having passed through the training of youth * * * without any religion, such seed as in them soon gets choked with the cares and pleasures of the world : these become open indifferentists, or else conform to Hindooism from motives of ease or interest. But many are too speculative, and many others have too much good in them to acquiesce in such a numbing of all the higher aspirations and sentiments of their nature, and these wandering hither and thither like sheep without a shepherd, incessantly beat the air in the vain pursuit after religious truth. A (very) few become Protestants, * * * A few become Atheists, and a few sceptics ; but, as a rule, Hindoos cannot get rid of their belief in a Supreme Government, and Theism decidedly prevails over Pantheism." With reference to the small school which professes allegiance to the doctrines of Comte, the Reviewer expresses an unfavorable opinion. He considers Positivism to be in no way adapted to the Hindoo mind, and that it is never likely to be more than a sickly exotic in India.

Before continuing our analysis of the article, we shall devote a few remarks to this last point.—It must be freely admitted that, at first sight, an almost impassable gulf does appear to be interposed between the Positivist mode of thought and the dreamy mysticism of Brahminical philosophy. The Hindoo, as a rule, is so thoroughly convinced not only of the reality but also of the supreme efficacy of his unsubstantial and visionary ideals that it is indeed difficult to see how he can be brought to that state of mental submission with respect to the mysteries of existence which Positivism so imperatively demands. But there is no reason for despair, since the laws of mental growth are the same everywhere, though the rates of progress may vary indefinitely according to varying circumstances of time or place. Sooner or later the logic of events must bring about, in India as well as in Europe, the substitution of the conception of Law for that of Will, and as a necessary consequence the substitution of a *human* for a *supernatural* point of view in all social and religious organisation.

The history of all great religious movements shows clearly enough that a system, when it has once been concentrated in a few eminent brains, is capable thereafter of almost indefinite extension. Now there cannot be a doubt that the teaching of Comte has deeply penetrated a few of the most select minds in Bengal. This is quite enough for the present. It is not desirable that Positivism should address itself, at the outset, to a very wide circle. For it is a system which is always misinterpreted by those who fail to master all its characteristic doctrines, and which, if accepted only for its scientific value, is sure to be perverted and made an instrument for increasing the already too prevalent corruption and disorder. The superficial advocate, the mere careless admirer is in truth far more to be deprecated than the most perverse adversary. The misrepresentation of foes is of little moment, as it can always be repelled; but the rash zeal of undisciplined partisans is not easily subdued, and may therefore work an incalculable amount of mischief. As Positivism does not appeal to men's fear of punishment or hope of reward during an eternal future, it can afford to wait. The old watchwords have served well enough for regulative purposes in times past, and they may continue to serve yet a little longer till Positivism has been able to organise in each of the most advanced nations, both of the West and the East, a small but powerful apostolate, a little band of disciples who can point to the salutary influence which their creed has exercised upon the heart as well as the intellect. No well established religious belief can ever perish until it is confronted with a morality superior to its own. Hence it cannot be expected that ordinary men should accept Positivism as their rule of life, until they have had some opportunity of seeing its moral efficacy displayed in practice.

A vast majority of educated Hindoos adopt Theism under some form or other, and in general manage to reconcile it with the ceremonial observances of a strictly orthodox Polytheism. Such a line of action is not necessarily hypocritical, since (as history clearly indicates) there is no direct antagonism between a belief in one Supreme Being ruling over a number of inferior powers, and a belief in several co-ordinate Deities each exercising sovereignty within certain vaguely defined limits. Some minds, however, unable to rest satisfied with any compromise between metaphysical Rationalism and orthodox Hindooism, deem it obligatory to enter a solemn protest against the popular creed, which they regard as at once false and mischievous. It is to such minds that Brahmoism owes its origin and development.

The Reviewer traces the history of Brahmoism, and discusses its peculiar tenets at length. As the subject is one which is thoroughly well known to all Indian readers it will not be necessary for us to do more than repeat the conclusions at which the Reviewer has arrived. " It is evident," he says, " that it (Brahmoism) is a mixed movement, partly conservative, moral, and religious, partly negative, rationalistic and self-sufficient. Between these two forces it is foundering, and must founder; and as this happens, many will go forward into scepticism, but many others, more predisposed for faith, will anxiously look around for some other refuge from infidelity. Catholicity, if properly explained to them, is precisely the system which such minds are in need of; and we venture to assert that if it were brought face to face with them, and if the scarecrow which is at present before their eyes as its representative were demolished, the day is coming when it could secure many most sincere and excellent converts, whose services as pioneers to their less-educated countrymen would be invaluable." With much of this we are inclined to agree, but we cannot persuade ourselves that Catholicism is at all likely to afford a refuge to more than a very insignificant fraction of those who will be anxious to escape from the disorder which must eventually arise, in the absence of any organic and authoritative creed. Any attempt on our part to prove the inefficacy of Catholicism would be out of place: what the future will bring forth can only be foreshadowed by a careful consideration of the present tendencies of human thought, and these tendencies appear to us to be completely adverse to the ultimate reception of any theological belief.

In conclusion we shall briefly indicate our own view of the Brahmic movement. Although not valuing much the so-called reforms of the Progressive School,*

---

* We feel convinced that the new school of Brahmoism, when considered from a religious point of view, can only spread among the lower or half educated classes by permitting a large admixture of the human element. There are already indications that the leader of this movement is being exalted by some of his followers to the rank of a prophet, if not of a mediator between God and man. However much the philosophical party, among the progressive Brahmos, may disclaim any wish to depart from a purely deistic type of worship, it is certain that their recent successes have been obtained t the expense of their theological metaphysics. Instead of trying to controvert this fact, it would be better if they faced it boldly and acknowledged the paramount necessity of grafting the human upon the divine. With a

we have the highest respect for the Brahmos as a body and especially for their distinguished and venerable chief Debendro Nath Tagore, a man endowed with no ordinary share of those peculiar gifts which enable their possessor to become a teacher and leader of the people. Brahmoism in the form which it has assumed under the guidance of Debendro Nath Tagore and his immediate co-adjutors is no doubt valuable as affording to many, who would otherwise be cast adrift upon the troubled waves of doubt, a religion which they can accept without difficulty, because it is the legitimate result of national modes of thought and action. We do not regard it as a definitive belief. Its metaphysical dogmas may assist its propagation among a certain class of minds, but the masses, we believe, require a less abstract creed and one that contains, under some form or other, a large infusion of the human element. Brahmoism, under whatever form it appears, makes two demands upon the intellect of the individual of such a nature that they can only be satisfied in a few exceptional cases. *First*, it requires each one to undertake a minute process of self-examination.† *Secondly*, it requires that the same result should be arrived at in every case.— Now men in general are so constituted that they prefer to take their beliefs upon trust, and not to work them out independently : they require teachers,

---

certain concession to the traditions of Hindooism, and a liberal infusion of the human element, Brahomism might become a most valuable provisional doctrine—enabling the nation to pass without confusion from the metaphysical to the positive stage.

† Brahmoism is not singular in thus appealing to the individual. In this respect it resembles the philosophy of Mr. J. S. Mill and his school. All such appeals the Positivist regards as utterly vicious. No thoroughly organic system can ever be established unless the individual is trained from infancy to the practice of reverence and submission, unless he is taught to look upon himself as a member of a vast community, and to draw the lessons which must guide his conduct not from the depths of his own inquisitive intellect, but from the stores of experience carefully accumulated by Humanity in the past.

men who speak with authority, as themselves divine, or as direct missionaries of a Higher Power, or as interpreters of the knowledge slowly accumulated by Humanity in the past. But even granting that each individual would consent to examine himself in order to elicit the requisite First Truths, what guarantee is there that the process would be correctly performed in every case, or that the same conclusions would be invariably arrived at? Of course so far as individuals can be induced to agree in their interpretations of self-consciousness, Brahmoism to that extent offers a basis of organisation: but it appears to us that such agreement must always be confined to a comparatively narrow circle of believers, and that Brahmoism therefore can never become a very formidable rival to any of the older religions.

———————ooo———————

4.—Dr. SIRCAR ON SCIENTIFIC EDUCATION.

A SMALL pamphlet has recently been published by Dr. Mahendra Lal Sircar, in which he advocates the establishment of a national institution for the cultivation of the Physical Sciences. We willingly admit with Dr. Sircar, that Physical Science ought, in the present day, to form a preponderating element in systematic education, but it appears to us that no clear or rational conception is formed by scientific thinkers, in general, with reference to the advantages that are to follow from the changes which they propose.

A new system of education is now required to meet the gradual change which is taking place in men's opinions— a change which must be followed sooner or later by a complete re-organisation of all our social institutions. The modification of our intellectual beliefs must not be regarded as an end in itself, but merely as preparatory to an improvement in our moral condition—for the intellect must ever be the servant and minister of the heart. The whole intellectual movement of modern times consists in a more or less conscious substitution of the notion of Law for that of Will in the regulation of all orders of phenomena. Now the chief benefit to be derived from a scientific training is, that the mind is enabled thereby to grasp effectually this idea of Law. When the majority of men have become thoroughly convinced that the reign of law is universal, they will dismiss the theological doctrine, of an arbitrary power controlling the world, as a fiction devoid henceforth of any regulative or organizing influence. It is in no way necessary for us to prove that the primitive conceptions are false. They have had an important value, both logically and scientifically, in past times, and no *a priori* reason can be given why they should not last for ever. It is experience alone which enables us to determine that a radical change of thought is taking place, but the evidence thus supplied is so overwhelming that we can afford to dispense with any other kind of proof. This change in our intellectual conceptions will necessarily involve a corresponding change in our feelings and actions. In considering the effects of a new system of education each of the three great elements of human nature ought to be taken into account, and it should always be carefully borne in mind that knowledge is valuable only so far as it may eventually lead to an improvement in man's moral condition. Scientific studies in themselves are rarely beneficial. They almost always foster pride and self-conceit, and, when too exclusively followed, have a very hardening influence upon the mind. To rob them of their danger they must be combined with a due culture of our moral and æsthetic faculties, and must be invariably pursued with a view to action, either immediate or remote.

Dr. Sircar has not examined in detail the course

of scientific study which he thinks it advisable to introduce. No doubt, however, he is fully aware how important it is that the reform, which he advocates, should be carried out on a rational and systematic plan. No good results can ensue unless the sciences are taught in a logical order, and with a definite end in view. A merely superficial acquaintance with some few isolated scientific facts would be of no value at all, if indeed it would not be positively injurious. As it is not our purpose to dwell upon this part of the subject at any length, we shall content ourselves with remarking that such an education, as the one contemplated by Dr. Sircar, cannot be efficiently organised unless it be made to rest upon a sound classification of our fundamental scientific conceptions. A classification admirably adapted for this purpose has been furnished by Comte in his Positive Philosophy.

What is required for the renovation of modern education is not a special study of one or more of the physical sciences, but the formation of a complete body of positive conceptions ranging over the whole field of human speculation. As Comte observes—

"The present exclusive speciality of our pursuits, and the consequent isolation of the sciences, spoil our teaching. If any student desires to form an idea of natural philosophy as a whole he is compelled to go through each department as it is taught, as if he were to be only an astronomer, or only a chemist; so that, be his intellect what it may, his training must remain very imperfect. And yet his object requires that he should obtain general positive conceptions of all the classes of natural phenomena. It is such an aggregate of conceptions, whether on a great or on a small scale, which must henceforth be the permanent basis of all human combinations. It will constitute the mind of future generations. In order to this regeneration of our intellectual system, it is necessary that the sciences, considered as branches from one trunk, should yield us, as a whole, their chief methods and their most important results. The specialities of science can be pursued by those whose vocation lies in that direction. They are indispensable; and they are not likely to be neglected; but they can never of themselves renovate our system of Education; and, to be of their full use, they must rest upon the basis of that general instruction which is a direct result of the Positive Philo-phy."

We have already stated that the change which is now taking place in our fundamental beliefs must eventually lead to a re-organisation of society. On this point also we cannot do better than produce the language of Comte. "Ideas" he says "govern the world, or throw it into chaos; in other words all social mechanism rests upon opinions. The great political and moral crisis that societies are now undergoing can be shown to arise out of intellectual anarchy. While stability in fundamental maxims is the first condition of genuine social order, we are suffering under an utter disagreement which may be called universal. Till a certain number of general ideas can be acknowledged as a rallying-point of social doctrine, the nations will remain in a revolutionary state, whatever palliatives may be devised; and their institutions can be only provisional. But whenever the necessary agreement on first principles can be obtained, appropriate institutions will issue from them, without shock or resistance; for the causes of disorder will have been arrested by the mere fact of the agreement. It is in this direction that those must look who desire a natural and regular, a normal state of society."

Dr. Sircar appears to be one of those who advocate the most unbounded liberty of thought and private judgment, yet strange to say he declares open war against prejudices of every description. Surely in a state of society where every individual is freely encouraged to form and retain his own opinions, prejudices, in any legitimate sense of the term, cannot be supposed to exist. Members of the individualist school, if they are consistent, must not brand with opprobrium *any* convictions, enlightened or otherwise, which are honestly entertained. Their system, at the best, is no doubt a suicidal one, but as propounded by Dr. Sircar its contradictory nature is at once manifest: for in the same sentence he not only condemns all restrictions upon liberty of thought, but also stigmatizes prejudices of every kind, whether they exist among priests or among men of science. Now, if there is to be that absolute freedom which Dr. Sircar contemplates, is not the prejudice of an ordinary man as much entitled to respect as the un-impassioned wisdom of an exceptional sage? "Ab-solute toleration of all opinions" says Dr. Sircar, "should mark civilization properly so called," never-theless he declares, that men cannot be said to have become civilized until they are free from all prejudice, or fearless of the consequences of discover-ies in the fields of knowledge. But when men have all reached that state of colourless neutrality so pleasing to minds of a certain order, and when therefore civilization, according to Dr. Sircar's view of it, is complete, what is there left for toleration to act upon? And even admitting that it is desirable for men to be thus thoroughly free from prejudice, how is this end to be attained where the right of private judgment is allowed to have all the binding force of a religious dogma? If no restrictions are to be imposed upon thought, the word *toleration* becomes meaningless. To *tolerate*, is to permit that which is not wholly approved. Hence in a commu-nity where freedom of thought is accepted as a fun-damental principle, it is nothing less than an insult for any one set of individuals to declare that they tolerate the opinions of any other set. We, as Posi-tivists, cannot admit that *toleration* is desirable as an end in itself. We do not indeed advocate persecu-tion or suppression of opinions by force, we do not suppress discussion, but we think it highly desirable that all our efforts should be directed towards one end—that end being, the annihilation of the existing intellectual anarchy by establishing a *consensus* in regard to the most vital questions that can interest mankind. This too appears to be the object of Dr. Sircar, although he does not explicitly admit it. The individualists always love to obscure their teachings with a cloud of revolutionary verbiage, but—conceal the fact as they may—it is really the unconscious yearning after a new and better faith which underlies the audacious negativism of all their characteristic doctrines. " If we look" says Comte " at what is the real meaning of the dogma of the universal and absolute right of inquiry, we shall find that it is the mere abstract expression of the temporary state of unbounded liberty in which the human mind was left by the decay of the theological philosophy, and which must last till the social advent of the positive philosophy. Negative as we now see this dogma to be, signifying release from old authority while waiting for the necessity of positive science—which already puts liberty of conscience out of the question in astronomy, physics, &c.,—the absolute character supposed to reside in it gave it energy to fulfil its revolutionary destination; enabled philosophers to explore the principles of a new organization; and, by admitting the right of all to a similar research, encouraged the discussion which must precede and effect the triumph of those principles. Whenever those principles shall have become established, the right of free inquiry will abide within its natural and permanent limits : that is, men will discuss under appropriate intellectual conditions, the real connection of various consequences with fundamental rules uniformly respected. Indispensable and salutary as it has been, this dogma can never be an organic principle. In any case private or public, the state of inquiry can evidently be only provisional, indicating the condition of mind which precedes and prepares for a final decision, towards which our reason is always tending, even when it is renouncing old principles, in order to form new ones. It is taking the exceptions for the rule when we set up, as a natural and permanent state, the precarious state which belongs to the period of transition ; and we ignore the deepest necessities of human reason when we would protract that scepticism which is produced by the passage from one mode of belief to another, and which is, in our need of fixed points of conviction, a kind of morbid perturbation which cannot be prolonged beyond the corresponding crisis whitout serious danger."

Dr. Sircar speaks of " the despotism of traditional opinions, opinions which have come down from the darkest ages, and which are still pertinaciously held by men who are no better than idlers, and who trifle with God's truth and with God's great gifts to man— his powers of observation and reasoning." Here then are some opinions which we presume Dr. Sircar is not disposed to tolerate, here are some truths which all men are bound to believe. It would have been well, however, if the learned doctor had given us some criterion for distinguishing between the truths which are of heaven and those which are of earth, for he cannot expect his countrymen to abandon their " unfounded opinions on all subjects" until they are furnished with definite rules by which they may test the nature of the doctrines which they are called upon to substitute for those which they have hitherto been trained to accept. Dr. Sircar says that " the Hindu religion, besides having in a pre-eminent degree the grand characteristic of all religions, which is to divorce the mind from the works of God, has besides become, through the corruptions of successive ages, a heterogeneous medley of theology, Philosophy, science, and what not,—in other words a chaotic mass of crude and undigested and unfounded opinions on all subjects, enunciated and enforced in the most dogmatic way imaginable."

Such language sounds somewhat strange from one who proclaims it to be a fundamental principle of his creed, that absolute toleration of *all* opinions should mark civilisation properly so called. Dr. Sircar while regarding all religions with a certain suspicion, manifests an undisguised contempt for the religion of Hindooism. Hence, even if unwilling to proscribe obnoxious opinions, he would, we imagine, prefer to dwell in a community where he was not called upon to tolerate the practices of a Polytheism which he regards as degrading and superstitious. As every religion, according to Dr. Sircar, divorces the mind of man from the works of God, religion itself cannot of course be reckoned by him among the works of God. But then we would ask him how it is that the Supreme Being allows so important a work as the formation and growth of man's religion to be carried on without his interference? Who is the mighty spiritual Potentate to whose care the religious development of man has been entrusted? By what name shall we call the Metaphysical Entity which has moulded into so many diverse forms the spiritual beliefs of the human race, those beliefs which have been regarded by such countless multitudes as the highest, the noblest, and the best of all the gifts with which they have been endowed? If Dr. Sircar wishes to make any deep impression upon his fellow-countrymen he must organise a more consistent creed than the one which he, at present, appears to hold: he must carry his positive science into every department of thought, and must not rest till he has thoroughly convinced himself that the fundamental idea of an immutable external order, upon which all science rests, is quite incompatible with any theological or metaphysical hypothesis as to the origin and destination of the world. A man cannot serve two masters: sooner or later, he must make his election between Theology and Positive Science. It is well known that

Dr. Sircar has not hesitated to display great courage and consistency in his professional career, we trust that he will advance with equal boldness in the region of speculation, and that he will see fit to carry out his scientific premises to their only legitimate conclusion. A mind like his can surely find but scant satisfaction amid the dregs of an effete metaphysical philosophy. We are inclined to think that in Positivism he would find a system admirably adapted to his wants. There would be no need for him, as a Positivist, to abandon that large spirit of liberality for which he evinces so hearty an admiration. On the contrary, he would find that in Positivism this spirit attains its fullest development, for Positivism alone is able to realize completely that noble maxim of the Catholic Church, *In necessary things unity; in doubtful things, liberty; in all things, charity.*

———ooo———

5.—THE CONTEMPORARY REVIEW ON POSITIVISM.

A REMARKABLE article appeared in the July (1868) number of the Contemporary Review, under the title ' Aspects of Positivism in relation to Christianity,' from the pen of an English clergyman, the Rev. Brooke F. Westcott. Although the writer does not accept Positivism as a whole, still it is evident that he fully appreciates its peculiar strength and value. The following extracts will serve not only to furnish an admirable exposition of the religious doctrines of Positivism, but also to indicate the powerful influence which those doctrines are, at present, exercising upon the theological world.

I. " Religion is" according to Comte " the complete harmony proper to human existence, individual and collective, when all its parts are brought into due relation to one another." It is for the soul, in other words, what health *is* for the body; and as health is essentially one, though in all cases variously and imperfectly realised, so too religion is essentially one, though it is attained in various forms and in different degrees. Even to the last, it is an ideal to which each specific type is an approximation.

The object of religion, corresponding to this definition, is set forth as two fold. It is destined at once to discipline the individual, and to unite the separate individuals in a harmonious whole. It aims at personal unity and social unity. And the same instincts which tend to correct the selfish instincts of each man, tend at the same time to bring all men into a true and lasting concord.

And as the aim of religion is twofold, so also is its base. It reposes on an objective, and on a subjective foundation. Without, there is the external order, in itself independent of us, which necessarily limits our thoughts and actions and feelings. Within, there is a principle of benevolent sympathy, which prompts us to look beyond our own wants and wishes, and to seek in a wider harmony the satisfaction of the deepest instincts of our nature.

The same dualism is extended also to the composition of religion. It has an intellectual part and a moral part. The former includes the adequate conception of the general laws of physics, of life, of society, to which our feelings and our actions are subordinated. The latter, under the shape of discipline, regulates our conduct at once public and private, and, under the shape of worship, guides and intensifies our feelings. Briefly, the sphere of doctrine is Thought, and its end is the True; the sphere of discipline is Action, and its end is the Good; the sphere of worship is Feeling, and its end is the Beautiful. And, as a whole, religion teaches us to know, to serve, and to love the Great Being, (Humanity,) in whom all that falls within the range of our powers is summed up.

II. Religion, Comte tells us, is the bringing into harmony the order without us and the spirit within us; the last and perfect combination of faith and love. This conception is the true key to his whole system. Our chief work, therefore, is to learn the character of the bases on which these final principles respectively repose.

On the one side then we have a vast external order, of which a fuller knowledge is gradually unfolded in the long course of ages, whereby we apprehend it as within certain limits at once fixed and variable. Step by step we are forced to contemplate the phenomena which it presents as falling into groups, and connected with one another by certain relations of sequence. The laws of observation which we thus form are extended gradually from physics to life, and from life to history, till we feel that not only are the ages permeated by "an increasing purpose" but that all being also is united by one principle. The efforts of Reason naturally culminate in the nobler efforts of Faith.

This order is apprehended, as has been said, as being both fixed and variable; and in both respects it affects us beneficently. The fixity furnishes a solid basis for our thoughts and actions, and, by making foresight generally possible, saves us from idle speculation and from misdirected energy. At the same time it sets an impassable limit to personal caprice, and, by basing all life upon submission, prepares men for sympathetic effort as united in obedince to a common supremacy. Its variability, on the other hand, is the pledge of progress. It stimulates speculation by suggesting a series of problems of surpassing interest. It guides activity by opening fields for labour, and substituting fruitful obedience for passive resignation. It represses at once asceticism and mysticism by offering its greatest blessings not to personal, but to social labour.

Such, according to Comte, is the objective basis of religion. On the other side, it is observed that there is an internal tendency in man, springing from benevolent affections, which carries him beyond himself in the search after his proper happiness and dignity. Just as the laws of the external world are only slowly and partially made known, so this inner life is brought out by the gradual evolution of society. The love of the Family passes into the love of the State; and the love of the State rises into the all-embracing love of Humanity.

This tendency also, like the external order, is at once fixed and variable. In some shape or other it will make itself felt in every man. It may be dwarfed and neutralised by atrophy, or strengthened and ennobled by exercise. But in its normal exercise Love spontaneously apprehends by moral intuition what Faith systematically constructs by intellectual processes; and at the last both coincide in their complete fulfilment. Faith sees the harmony of all things, which Love feels.

Nor may we forget that while the ultimate objective and subjective bases of religion are thus broadly distinguished, there is yet always a human element in our conception of the cosmos, and a cosmical element in our feelings as men. The unity of the world is subjective. The laws of phenomena are gained by the abstraction of the constant part from the variable. And conversely, the development of love is objective. It gains strength only as it is manifested according to the conditions of our existence. Man indeed is himself, according to the wise instinct of old philosophers, a microcosm, including in his own person the action of all the laws which we observe without us, and supplementing them by that higher law of love whereby he alone is capable of religion.

According to this exposition, it is evident that religion is built upon knowledge, and the Positivist system of doctrine is simply the outline of the hierarchy of the sciences, which are severally subordinated one to another, and each regulated by its peculiar laws. In due succession the believer or the student—for the words become synonymous—learns to appreciate the universal laws of number, time, and space, by which all our definite conceptions are ruled; next he passes to those of physics, which are more complicated and less general; then to those of chemistry, which bring him to the verge of life. The investigation of the laws of life leads to that of the laws of society; and the last and crowning science in this scheme is that of morals.

Such an encyclopædic view of the great departments of knowledge reveals two important principles. Each science is based upon those which precede it in the scale, so that in every case the nobler phenomena are subordinated to the lower. And, secondly, each science, as it increases in complexity, admits also of greater variations. To these principles two corollaries may be added. First that each series of laws produces its full effect in every instance though the result may be modified by the action of new forces acting according to new laws. And, again that the power of foresight which measures the definiteness of the law, varies from absolute certainty in the case of combinations of number, and the like, to indefinite doubt when we speculate on the isolated action of individuals.

III. The ideas which are thus brought into prominence are those of continuity, solidarity and totality.

(1) *The idea of continuity.*—A very little reflection will show the profound influence which continuity exercises upon life. When it is once apprehended, no religion which claims to be universal

can neglect it. Materially, intellectually, and morally, we are the children of the past, destined in turn to give birth to a new race which will inherit all that we possess. Whatever view we may take of the originative power of the individual, and we claim necessarily that the personal will shall be admitted to be an independent force, it is evident that the accumulations of wealth of every form which furnish the instruments of our action, the treasures of language which control the general tenour of our thoughts, the forms and habits of social and national intercourse which stimulate and guide our feelings, are incomparably stronger than any individual power which can be brought to bear upon them. If it were not so, in place of society we should have chaos. And all these are in their source and growth independent of us. We can watch how, in old times, the various results of labour and reflection and conflict were gathered up and perpetuated in abiding shapes; but we have no choice but to receive them. It is our privilege to modify, but not to begin. More and more as the ages go on, in Comte's striking phrase, we who live are ruled by the dead, though it is our prerogative to serve them with a free and willing service, and in our turn, when our work is done, to be joined with them in the sovereignty of the future.

Two important conclusions flow from this law of our earthly existence. The first is, that progress is the development of order; and the second, that the thoughts or institutions of the past can be applied to the present only by a method of proportion.

No one looking back over the past can fail to detect a general advance of humanity, as a whole, in certain definite directions corresponding to what we observe in the fuller development of the man. The progress, on a large scale, exhibits the harmonious elevation of our whole complex being, even though periods of devastation and fiery trial are needed for the preparation of the future growth.

The second consequence, though it is really more obvious, is more commonly overlooked. Any expression of popular judgment, whether it be made by word or by act, is necessarily relative to the time and circumstances under which it is made. As circumstances change, it does not by any means follow that the changes in the acceptation of words or in the significance of acts will be made in the same direction, so that the relation between them will remain fixed. And therefore, if we would gain for ourselves the blessings which we can refer in past ages to certain institutions or formulas, it can only be by realising the relation in which they stood to the whole of society then, and finding their proportional representatives now.

(2) *The idea of solidarity.*—The doctrine of solidarity is not less fruitful of thought than that of continuity. It presents to us (if such an illustration is allowable) in a horizontal section a similar succession of varieties of society to that which we have considered there in a vertical section. Or, to take another mode of expression, it presents in the extension of space what continuity regards in the extension of time. In a family, or a city, or a nation, we can readily apprehend how the co-existing members are bound together so as to form a whole, of which each part is really, though remotely, united to the other by material and moral actions and reactions. Our observation of the subtle influences by which continuity is preserved helps us to extend this idea yet further. Nation is thus seen to be moved by nation, stock by stock, till the whole race which is connected spiritually by a community of nature, is felt also to be connected actually by mutual, though often indirect, operations of each fragment upon the rest.

Whenever we seize, however tremblingly, as at best it must be, this vast conception of the Great Being in which all mankind is for the time united, it is evident that our views of the destiny, of the relations, and of the action of men will be greatly influenced. The thought which inspires hope, and assures patience, at the same time ennobles labour, and stimulates action. Hope and patience spring necessarily out of the application of the lessons of the past to the present. We can see how rivalries and conflicts, the rise and fall of principles and states, the very exhaustion of powers once beneficent and life-giving, have contributed to the whole progress of human life. We can believe then that phenomena of the kind, when co-existent, are no less instrumental of good. And it is no objection to this faith that it is not in our experience converted into sight. Life would be indefinitely impoverished if the fruits of effort or suffering were not reserved in the richest measure for the future.

The present effect of the idea of solidarity upon labour and action is perhaps less frequently realised than the remoter effect which has been just noticed, but it is at least capable of being far more energetic. Briefly, it may be summed up in two principles. It consecrates the permanent variety of functions in life, and substitutes duties for rights.

As long as we regard individuals as so many separate units, it is clear that we must regard complete equality as the ultimate ideal of their state. The object of reform must be to assimilate man to man. But this chimerical fancy loses all rational basis when the individual is seen to be the member of a body which itself is part of a greater whole, of which the final dimensions surpass all human imagination. Then it follows at once that complexity of office is the condition of health. The completeness of health depends on the completeness of the organism. Society, in every true sense, would cease to exist with-out an abiding distinction of classes. Humanity would be poorer if it were deprived of any national or specific types. There is no confusion in the mul-tiplicity of service. There is no levelling, no dis-paragement in the just subordination of distinct works. The essential variety, the actual combination, both belong to the characteristics of life.

And if we apply the principle to the separate works of each, it becomes, as it were, a revelation of the moral dignity of labour. No one in any society works for himself. Each worker is a servant of the body. He does really co-operate with all for the good of all. It is only required that he should feel the destination, and the source of what he re-ceives. Then at last he would, as Comte admirably expresses the truth, know that " live *for* others" is but another aspect of "living *by* others"

At the same time the transference of our point of sight from the individual to the body brings out into clear light the second principle. If the indivi-dual be the centre, then he may have rights; but if the body be the centre, he can have only duties.

(3.) *The idea of totality.*—The doctrine of totality carries yet one step further the doctrines of con-tinuity and solidarity. It is not only that the suc-cessive generations of men are linked together by laws which they can only modify, and not abrogate, nor yet that each generation is interpenetrated and united by a common life; but the life of humanity is itself ruled, in a great measure, by the medium in which it is passed. The influence of physical pow-ers upon man may have been exaggerated, but we cannot deny that it is real. Comte himself does not overstate it. " The world," he writes, " furnishes the materials, and man determines the form." " Man is not a result of the world, and yet he depends upon it." The observed variations of nature and man are not sufficient to disturb our confidence in the fixity of what we call natural laws. And, conversely, while the laws remain fixed, man is so far capable of modifying the elements through which their action is displayed, as to seriously alter their total effect. If again we regard only living forms, here the power of man is supreme. Some die away at his approach; others follow him; others are capable of receiving what we are forced to call the moral impress of his character.

To pursue in any detail the consequences which flow from this connection of man with the physical world would be impossible here. It must be enough to notice the general lessons which it teaches as to the action of man and the destiny of creation. As to the first, it shows that the sovereignty of man is manifested, not in the direct exertion, but in the guidance of force. The effect in each case depends not so much on power as on wisdom. In other words, our true strength lies in taking each discovered law as the rule according to which we may employ our energies, always remembering that the higher phenomena rest upon and include the lower, and are modifiable in direct proportion to their complexity.

On the other hand, as man is at present continually modifying all nature, both spontaneously and of purpose, it is necessary to regard the connection thus established as in some sense permanent. We cannot wholly sever the fate of the lower and humbler companions of man, for example, from the fate of man himself. And perhaps there is nothing more characteristic of Comte than the almost importunate eagerness with which he claims for the animals which habitually co-operate with man, to assure his worthy objects, incorporation, according to their individual dignity and services, in the Great Being into which man himself passes."

III.—LETTERS TO THE EDITOR OF THE BENGALEE.

1.—POSITIVISM AND ATHEISM.

SIR,—We are glad to find that you have of late opened your columns to the discussion of that peculiar phase of opinion, termed Positivism, which is now so well-known in Europe and which is, we think, peculiarly adapted to win the sympathy of the best intellects in India at a period like the present when the supports, upon which the complex fabric of Hindoo Society has so long rested, are slowly giving way, threatening destruction and ruin in their fall.

It cannot, however, be denied that, in giving a hearing to Positivism, you are exposing yourself to the charges usually brought against its fundamental principles—charges inaccurate indeed, but still such as to demand consideration.

One of the most ordinary objections, and the only one to which we shall now allude, is that Positivism is simply Atheism. Whatever conclusion may be arrived at by those who carefully study the system, it should be remembered that Comte himself always strenuously repudiated the distinctive tenets of Atheism. The term 'Atheist' has a definite and well known signification; it implies one who *denies* the existence of a First Cause, and asserts the eternity of matter. Hence it is manifest that Atheism offers a solution of those peculiar problems with which the metaphysician deals, that it is in fact one aspect of the metaphysical stage. Now Positivism gives up the search after causes either First or Final, it restricts man to the world of phenomena, and concerning the extra-phenomenal, it neither affirms nor denies.

From the first dawn of speculation man has been attempting to answer certain questions to which no satisfactory reply has yet been given, no reply which *all* can agree to regard as definite. Does not this repeated failure, it may be asked, indicate the fruitlessness of the attempt? But though no advance has been made in that weird region which stretches beyond the empire of human reason, there is a field in which man has been pre-eminently successful, and on which he has gained the most signal triumphs, namely, the field of positive science : there results have been obtained which are unanimously accepted, which amidst all the misery and confusion that still prevail, have been instrumental in conferring not a few solid benefits upon our race, and which ever widening give promise of the day when " the kindly earth shall slumber, lapt in universal Law."

The most strenuous opponents of Positivism can hardly deny that metaphysical speculation remains in much the same condition that it was of old among Vedic commentators and Greek philosophers, that the same questions are ever recurring and the same antagonistic solutions are being constantly given by opposite schools, who support their respective views by fruitless controversy and sometimes by unseemly recrimination : nor can they deny that science has been steadily advancing from the earliest ages when men first gazed with mingled awe and curiosity on the starry heavens, till now when the belief is becoming general that all events are subject to the sway of inflexible law.

Be it understood, however, that while Positivism pronounces the labours of the metaphysician to be *ultimately* fruitless, it does not regard those labours in the past as useless. The enquiry into causes was natural at first, and necessary in order to stimulate mental activity ; it was only by attempting to penetrate the hidden secrets of nature that the barrenness of the task could be rendered manifest, at the same time the attempt was provisionally beneficial as affording an outlet for the highest mental activity, and as presenting a transitional doctrine which effected a kind of synthesis until the conception of a positive philosophy could emerge from the complete ensemble of the Sciences. The metaphysical stage is also essential in order thoroughly to undermine the supernatural theory. An immediate substitution of positive for theological conceptions being impossible, an intervening stage is required during which the dogmas of theology are abandoned and the precepts of science partially disregarded, during which matters of faith are submitted to reason, while reason itself is done violence to, so as to afford what is deemed a rational solution of mysteries which, when withdrawn from the province of faith, become mere empty formulæ—divested of all that power to influence conduct which they so admirably exerted at the commencement of the theological regime.

I am, Sir,

Yours obediently,

A POSITIVIST.

2.—THE AIM OF POSITIVISM.*

SIR,—As the notices which you have hitherto published on Positivism, regard the system from a purely scientific point of view, it may not be out of place to indicate briefly the ultimate aim of a philosophy which must not be estimated by its scientific value alone.

There are many at the present time whose minds are in a purely negative condition, who would nevertheless gladly embrace some definite opinions if they could only meet with a system which would enable them to harmonise all the elements of human nature. These elements will be found to be disunited in every community where the Metaphysical Philosophy has triumphed over the primitive beliefs. So long as the old Theology was willingly accepted, it was possible to unite under one government Feeling, Intellect and Action. But so soon as the Intellect began to call in question the fundamental theological dogmas, this union was dissolved; and the estrangement between Feeling on the one hand and Intellect on the other grew wider and wider till open war was declared between them. Man's Action, being guided partly by Feeling and partly by Intellect, was necessarily affected by the change which thus took place in the relations between the two governing elements. In the West, and in those parts of the East which have been most influenced by Western

---

* This letter has been considerably modified since it appeared in the Bengalee.

teaching, this conflict has proceeded almost as far as it can without actually destroying the bonds which hold society together. There are some amiable persons who, thoroughly aware of the disorder which exists, attempt to patch up a hollow truce by declaring that Faith and Reason are quite distinct, and even incompatible, so that the latter has no right whatever to interfere within the dominions of the former. Positivism discards all such futile expedients; it endeavours to show how Faith and Reason may be reconciled, how the same general principles may be made to govern every department of human energy. Hence it commends itself to the attention of all who cannot rest content with principles which are merely destructive, which would lead to the exaltation of reason at the expense of Faith, or to the securing for Faith an unnatural triumph over Reason. Under existing theological conditions an equal alliance between Faith and Reason is impossible: when attempted, it only leads to incongruous results. This is well manifested in the struggle which Protestantism carries on with Catholicism: the Protestant gives ample scope to Reason when his object is to undermine the legends and dogmas of his adversary, yet when his own system is attacked he shrinks from the application of the same negative criticism which has served him so well as a weapon of offence, but which he will not allow to be wielded within that restricted and arbitrary boundary which, according to him, limits the realm where Faith must reign supreme. To minds of a certain type this procedure may be satisfactory, but there are many who cannot appreciate it, and who crave a method which they can regard as thoroughly consistent. This desire of consistency gives rise to two separate classes, one clinging to the primitive theology which has the merit of being logical and systematic, the other, (which is simply negative,) abandoning all idea of any permanent union between the seemingly hostile powers which contend for the empire of the human mind. Positivism addresses itself more especially to the latter class, providing them with a definite system, and presenting to their view a banner round which their scattered forces may rally, and in defence of which they may securely advance to the conflict that awaits them. It cannot be denied that the claims of

Positivism are exacting, and whether it is really justified in making such claims time alone can show : it appeals to the test of experience, and by this test it must stand or fall. The essential points are these : *first*, that a gradual change is taking place in our conception of the universe, the notion of law being everywhere substituted for that of external and arbitrary agency ; *secondly*, that all our knowledge is phenomenal, and that when we endeavour to advance beyond the world of phenomena we become involved in hopeless confusion and inconsistency ; *thirdly*, that henceforward the necessary conditions of stability can only be secured by organising society upon an exclusively human basis.

If these premises can be maintained, it must follow that society will eventually undergo a thorough renovation, and whether the change takes place in accordance with the plan traced out by Comte, or in some other less systematic manner, is immaterial so far as the final result is concerned. A theory of some kind, however, is absolutely necessary as a guide for action. The organising power of theology has been long extinct, the metaphysical theories have been tried and found wanting; we are forced, therefore, by the logic of events to adopt henceforward a human stand-point. Admitting this, Positivism immediately recommends itself to our notice as a theory at once clear, comprehensive, and consistent, and as admirably adapted to rally into one united phalanx all who have abandoned the old beliefs and yet can see no hope of safety in the discordant doctrines of the existing liberal or revolutionary schools.

I am, Sir,

Yours obediently,

A Positivist.

3.—(a) POSITIVISM NOT DEISM.*

(b) HINDOO THEOLOGISM.

SIR,—(a) If Professor Bhattacharjea believes that Comte intended to sanction Deism as a definitive doctrine, because he preferred the hypothesis of an *intelligent will* to that of *blind chance* in the works of nature, we must respectfully beg to observe that, in our opinion, the learned professor is completely mistaken.† Whatever Mr. Mill or others may say to the contrary we feel convinced that no compromise is possible between Deism and Positivism. The origin and destination of the world are mysteries which never can be penetrated by man. This is the most fundamental tenet. Those who cannot cheerfully accept it are not likely, as a rule, to give up their prejudices against Comte; nor is it desirable that they should, for no beneficial results are likely to follow unless Positivism is accepted as a whole. The true Positivist must be content to build upon a simply human basis; and if he accepts the doctrine of Humanity with " a meek and quiet spirit" he will find that he has obtained an ideal which is fully worthy to replace the noblest abstractions of the past.

(b.) Professor Bhattacharjea has alluded, in his letter, at some length, to the intricate and ingenious nature of Hindoo Pantheism. Now since the learned professor is so well acquainted with the philosophy of Comte and is at the same time so distinguished for his knowledge of Sanskrit literature, he would, we should presume, be eminently well-qualified for undertaking a task which will never

---

* This letter has been considerably modified.

† This refers to a letter addressed, by Professor Krishna Kamal Bhattacharjea, to the Editor of the Bengalee (October 5th, 1867.) In this letter the Professor dwelt at some length on the metaphysical ingenuity displayed by the authors of the Upanishads, and argued that, as Comte had expressed himself strongly against Pantheism, there was no occasion to be prejudiced against him on account of his Atheism. Comte was of opinion that the Order of Nature is far more compatible with the hypothesis of an intelligent will than that of a blind mechanism. This, according to Professor Bhattacharjea, is enough to silence the uneasy feelings of those who are shocked by a religion without God. Theists whose feelings can be thus easily silenced are surely not as wise as serpents, although they may be as harmless as doves.

be accomplished so long as the investigation of the earliest historical records is undertaken only by the Metaphysical School.
That task is—To describe the process by which Hindoo Pantheism
was gradually developed out of the old popular creed; or,—in more
precise terms,—to trace the growth of Hindooism from a state of
pure Fetichism in the earliest ages until it was transformed into
the Metaphysical Philosophy of a comparatively recent period.

Hitherto it has generally been the custom to assume a primitive age in which the belief in pure monotheism was universally
prevalent, and to suppose that men, in some way which is not
explained, lapsed into fetichism, astrolatry, and polytheism, all of
which are included under the one comprehensive term 'idolatry.'
Max Muller, in his History of Sanskrit literature, endorses this
theory, and endeavours to show that the Vedic hymns contain a
germ of pure monotheism. That they should contain such a germ
is not surprising as among the sages of the Vedic period some
few had doubtless advanced beyond the prevailing popular conceptions: but the general tendency of these hymns is decidedly
polytheistic, and indicative of an earlier fetichistic phase of belief
from which the national mind had not long emerged.

The theories of the Metaphysical School would receive their
death-blow if some competent Sanskrit scholar should succeed in
drawing out from the Vedas that vein of latent Fetichism which
runs through them; and in showing, with some degree of probability, how the transition was effected from pure nature-worship to
the adoration of those bright and beautiful deities who presided
over the elements as they appeared to the simple faith and wonder-
ing gaze of India's sons more than thirty centuries ago.*

---

* There is a striking correspondence between the early Hindoo and Greek
mythologies. They both, moreover, bear a similar relation to the later developments of the popular creed. In each case the earliest divinities are eminently
concrete,—they seem to be almost confounded with the objects which they per-
sonify, and are far removed from that distinctively human type which obtained,
during a later age, both in India and Greece. Okeanus, Gæa, and such like
deities, bear the same relation to Zeus and the other Gods of Olympus, that
Varuna, Prithivi, and such-like, bear to Vishnu, Siva, and their peers. In each
case the earlier pantheon represents a stratum of theological belief which has
been recently superimposed upon the primary Fetichism, and which in its turn is

Of course it cannot be expected that the different elements should ever be completely separated. Fetichism and Theologism have always been more or less intermixed throughout all *historical* periods. Pure Fetichism can only be found either among the lower animals and infants, or among tribes extremely low in the scale of civilisation. But it never altogether perishes, though it is modified more and more as the human mind advances in its growth. Great care, therefore, would be required in discriminating between the theistic and fetichistic elements; and for this reason alone, any historical investigation ought to be undertaken by a native of India who is thoroughly well acquainted with all the social and religious institutions of his country, and who is able to sympathise with the feelings and prejudices of every class in the community to which he belongs.

A specimen of the successful application of Positive principles to such questions has been lately furnished by M. Laffitte in his Essay on Chinese Civilisation. This little treatise would form an excellent guide to any native Sanskrit scholar who would undertake to trace out, as we have suggested, the gradual development of Hindoo Polytheism.

I am, Sir,

Yours obediently,

A Positivist.

4.—ON MIRACLES.

Sir,—Three articles have lately appeared in the *Bengalee* on the subject of Miracles. The writer appears to be a man of little faith, yet, in his third article, he has made certain assumptions which, if granted, would establish the intelligibility of miraculous agency, and by allowing the fact of one miracle would imply the possibility of all others.

---

overlaid by a fully-developed Polytheism, in which the objects of worship are endowed wtih well-defined attributes and a marked individuality. It will be observed that the gradual advance from the concrete to the abstract is precisely similar in both these cases.

Surely no miracle can be more stupendous than the *creation* of the universe. Yet many who are unwilling to admit the possibility of miraculous agency in support of any revealed religion, do not hesitate to accept this vast infraction of that most stringent law of nature *Ex nihilo nihil fit.* If the creation of the world is intelligible, surely it must be quite as intelligible that a supernatural influence could restore to life a single dead body. Either Divine power is an hypothesis employed to veil our ignorance, or it is a *vera causa.* If the former is the case, it should be *altogether* discarded when its artificial nature is rendered manifest; but if the latter is the correct view, we cannot object to the general principle of miracles, though we may, for good reasons, discard this or that particular miracle. The difficulty in believing a miracle is not surmounted by withdrawing special and particular cases from the immediate influence of the Divine Energy, and restricting that Energy to the creation of some whole or complete organisation. Once introduce supernatural agency, and you cannot consistently limit it to a narrow sphere— it must operate universally and in a manner which reason cannot comprehend. The objection that " with God all things are possible," seems a perfectly valid one against those who assume the existence of God, and who at the same time bind him down to work merely in accordance with their own preconceived notions. Herein we have displayed the inherent vice of all metaphysical conceptions —the details of theology are repudiated but the basis is retained. Now if you accept the basis, you cannot consistently reject the details which rest upon it. Either we must frankly accept one of the many existing theologies, or we must altogether discard the supernatural. We can still humbly and reverently recognise the mystery of existence, even though we cease from attempting to penetrate secrets which, prolonged experience has taught us, are for ever hidden from our view.

I am, Sir,

Yours obediently,

A POSITIVIST.

5.—REV. K. S. MACDONALD ON COMTE.

Sir,—In the report of the Rev. Mr. Macdonald's lecture on
Comte, (which appeared in the *Indian Daily News* of July 23rd,)
the following passage occurs :—"It was immediately on his rupture with St. Simon that he set up what he called the Positive
Philosophy, and which he published to the world in 1822 and 1825,
in his Essays called, respectively, 'A plan concerning the essentials
to the re-organising of society,' and 'Philosophic considerations
concerning the sciences and the savans.'" As this passage is
somewhat ambiguous and might convey to many an erroneous
impression, we think it advisable to state the facts connected with
this portion of Comte's life more explicitly.

Comte joined St. Simon in 1818, when he was 20 years of age;
the connection lasted till 1824, thus extending over a period of 6
years. During this time Comte published the following essays :—

(1.) *General separation between opinions and desires.* (1819.)

(2.) *A summary appreciation of the general character of past
modern history.* (Published in 1820, in the *Organisateur*, and
attributed to St. Simon.)

(3.) *A plan of the scientific labours requisite for organising
society.* (Printed for the first time in 1822, in a pamphlet entitled
Du Contrat Social, written by St. Simon. Reprinted in 1824,
in the *Catechisme des industriels.*)

The third is the most important of these early works. When
first published in 1822 the name of Comte was not affixed to it
out of regard to the religious opinions of his parents. But when
it was reprinted, in 1824, in St. Simon's *Catechisme*, Comte
objected to the anonymous form of publication, and it was because
St. Simon would not listen to the remonstrances of his young
colleague that the rupture took place between them.

As the germs of the Positive Philosophy may be discovered
in this essay, it is scarcely correct to maintain, without some
qualification, that he only set up what he called the Positive
Philosophy immediately on his rupture with St. Simon. The
celebrated law of the three stages was first enunciated in this essay,
and upon this law hinges the whole of the Positive Philosophy.

Grant but this fundamental principle, and one can scarcely refuse to follow Comte to the most important of the conclusions at which he has arrived by its aid.

We shall not discuss the point as to whether Comte really was the discoverer of the law or not, believing as we do that he has fully made good his claim to be its real author, inasmuch as he is the only one who has drawn from it its necessary consequences, the only one who has succeeded in building upon it a consistent and luminous system. If it existed in the mind of any man previous to Comte it could have been but as a happy guess, and not as a fruitful principle, or legitimate generalisation from all the facts of history.

The Rev. Mr. Macdonald observes that "in 1842 Comte separated from his wife, and soon after entertained a passionate love for the wife of a galley slave." The lady thus alluded to as 'the wife of a galley slave,' is the now celebrated Madame Clotilde de Vaux, whose husband though respectably connected and occupying a good social position, committed an offence which brought him under the grasp of the law and led to his being condemned to the galleys for life. Madame de Vaux being young, beautiful and accomplished, the philosopher when introduced to her was easily vanquished. The admiration was mutual, though on the part of the lady it appears to have sprung rather from the enthusiasm of the disciple, than from the fond attachment of the lover. From the first Madame Clotilde de Vaux gave Comte to understand that the connection between them must partake simply of the character of an exalted friendship. Comte not unwillingly acquiesced in the lady's views, and was rejoiced that at length he had found a woman who was both willing and qualified to become a disciple. This lady, as Mr. Macdonald justly observes, exercised the greatest influence upon Comte's subsequent life and labours,—on his works, sociology, and religion. But some of the followers of Comte will not be inclined to agree with Mr. Macdonald when he says, that the philosopher now threw overboard his own philosophy, discarded his positive method and created a magnificent utopia in the religion of humanity. There is no doubt that Madame de Vaux exercised a most potent influence over the mind of Comte, and that all his speculations after the eventful year 1842, are tinged with an exaltation of feeling which we look for in vain among the sober pages of the 'Philosophie Positive.' In spite however of the change of style and a certain lofty enthusiasm which strikes the reader in Comte's later writings, there is still no deviation from the strictly positive method, which is deductive as well as inductive and which admits, under certain essential restrictions, of any hypotheses that are consistent with all the ascertained data. A Positive Polity had been clearly traced out in the Philosophy; and Comte, from the very first, had insisted upon the necessity of a new doctrine which should thoroughly renovate man, intellectually, socially and morally. The magnificent dream of his youth was but realised in his maturity—the dicta of the philosopher being transformed into the dogmas of the apostle, the stern calculations of the man of science into the jubilant gospel of the prophet. Even if we grant, with Mr. Macdonald, that Comte's Religion *is* a magnificent Utopia, yet the author of that religion would still appear to us to be deserving of all praise for his bold attempt and thorough consistency. The whole tendency of modern thought and action goes to prove that society must eventually be constituted upon a purely human basis, and when men apply themselves consciously to the work of reconstruction they will doubtless feel grateful to Comte for the valuable suggestions which, in his later works, he has furnished for the aid of those who are engaged in such a task.

In order to place the connection between Comte and Madame de Vaux upon its proper footing, we adduce the following passage from the preface to the Catechism. "Whilst she (Madame de Vaux) lived I had felt her angelic influence for one year only. She has now for more than six years, since her death, been associated with all my feelings. Through her I have at length become for humanity, in the strictest sense, a twofold organ, as may any one who has reaped the full advantages of woman's influence. My career had been that of Aristotle—I should have wanted energy for that of St. Paul, but for her. I had extracted sound philosophy from real science; I was enabled by her to found on the basis of that philosophy the universal religion. The perfect parity of our connexion, which circumstances made exceptional, and even the admirable superiority of the angel who never received her due recognition—on these I need not dwell—they are already fully appreciated by the nobler order of minds. * * * *

"Superior as she was, Madame Clotilde de Vaux was yet so early taken from me as to render it impossible sufficiently to initiate her in Positivism, naturally the object of all her wishes and efforts. Even before death broke off finally the work of affectionate instruction, pain and grief had been very serious impediments. I was hardly able to sketch out to her whilst alive the systematic preparation which I now accomplish with her when dead."

With regard to Comte's insanity, if it had any influence at all upon his writings, we are of opinion that Mr. Macdonald's theory is preferable to any other which has been yet propounded. That theory is, that inasmuch as germs of his later extravagances are to be found in *all* his works, and inasmuch as from his boyhood he was distinguished by a chronic irritability, a most passionate despotism and a most extraordinary precocity—he must have been suffering at *all times* from a diseased brain. Genius it is said is akin to madness, to us it seems that what Mr. Macdonald would call Comte's madness was wondrously akin to genius.

I am, Sir,

Yours obediently,

August 8, 1868.   A POSITIVIST.

6.—DIVORCE.*

SIR,—IN your article, of last Saturday, on the " Brahmo Marriage Bill," certain strictures were made upon Comte's theory of marriage, which appear to involve some misapprehension as to the aim and scope of the Positive Sociology.

------

* This letter has been altogether remodelled since it appeared in the Bengalee.

It is perfectly correct to describe Comte as indulging in "enthusiastic aspirations after moral elevation." The moral part of man's nature is, according to Comte, the highest and noblest; intimately dependent indeed on the other parts for its support and growth, but at the same time coordinating those parts and ruling over them in virtue of its superior authority and worth. But it should be remembered that this complete supremacy of the moral element is an ideal, to which it is desirable that a near approximation should be made in practice, but which we can never expect to be fully realised. Comte has amply provided for this schism between the ideal and the real by the total separation of the spiritual and temporal powers : one great object of the temporal power being to diminish and control the rigour of the spiritual power.

As Marriage is one of the most valuable social institutions which we have inherited from the theological *regime*, Comte has adopted every possible precaution in order to secure its permanence and to maintain its efficacy. For this purpose he has retained the religious sanction of theology in a form adapted to the Positive mode of thought, and has insisted, (from a *theoretical* point of view,) on the desirability of rendering the marriage indissoluble *even by death.** But while thus indicating the course which he deemed most suitable in order to realise the full perfection of man's nature, he knew well enough that human frailty would render a rigid application of his theory impossible. Hence side by side with the higher sanctions of religion he allows the purely secular sanctions of the state to flourish. In spite of its revolutionary origin he has adopted the institution of civil marriage, expressly in order to guarantee liberty in the performance of prescriptions which are purely religious. A ratification of the marriage contract before a Civil Magistrate is necessary in every case ; it must be moreover sufficient in those cases where the parties concerned are not willing to satisfy the purely moral obligations of the religious code.

* "It develops the principle of monogamy, by inculcating, not as a legal institution, but as a moral duty, the perpetuity of widowhood." *General View of Positivism.* p. 254.

Speaking of Divorce he says—" St. Augustine, overcoming by his own unaided reason the necessarily absolute character of his theological belief, opens his chief work by remarking that murder may often be excusable, and, at times, even praiseworthy. The same may be said of falsehood, and of every thing else that generally deserves reprobation. Divorce is no exception to this general rule. But whilst we allow this we must never impair the fundamental indissolubility of the marriage tie. There is in reality but one case in which marriage may be dissolved by law, the case where one or other of the parties has been condemned to any such degrading punishment as to be socially dead. In all other cases of disturbance, a long continuance of unworthy conduct on the part of husband or wife may lead to moral disruption of the union, the result of which is a separation, but without allowing a second marriage. Positive religion imposes on the innocent in such cases the observance of chastity, but the recognition of that obligation is compatible with the deepest affection. If the condition is felt to be hard, it must be submitted to, primarily in the interest of social order; then, as the just consequence of the original error."

Such views will doubtless appear far too rigid to those who are anxious that the limits of divorce should be widened to the utmost. But if it be conceded that marriage offers the highest type of social union, and that it is desirable to retain the respect for this institution unimpaired,—then every safeguard should be carefully preserved, and all attacks upon its integrity should be vigorously repelled. By endeavoring to destroy the sanctity of marriage the revolutionary school are undermining one of the noblest social bulwarks raised by the faith and devotion of their ancestors. It is indeed strange to see how the members of this school persist in rejecting the most salutary rules and prescriptions of the past, while they willingly do homage to its chief intellectual fictions—fictions whose sole merit, to a Positivist, consists in the social and moral results which have been achieved by their aid.

The evil consequences of the unrestrained practice of Divorce were clearly exhibited at Rome in the days of the Empire. The following passage from Gibbon, (a writer who cannot be charged with visionary or despotic tendencies) may perhaps command the respectful attention of many who would not hesitate to reject the so-called utopias of Comte :—" When the Roman matrons became the equal and voluntary companions of their lords, a new jurisprudence was introduced, that marriage, like other partnerships, might be dissolved by the abdication of one of the associates. In those centuries of prosperity and corruption, this principle was enlarged to frequent practice and pernicious abuse. Passion, interest or caprice, suggested daily motives for the dissolution of marriage ; a word, a sign, a message, a letter, the mandate of a freedman, declared the separation ; the most tender of human connections was degraded to a transient society of profit or pleasure. According to the various conditions of life, both sexes alternately felt the disgrace and the injury : an inconstant spouse transferred her wealth to a new family, abandoning a numerous, perhaps a spurious, progeny to the paternal authority and care of her late husband ; a beautiful virgin might be dismissed to the world, old, indigent, and friendless ; but the reluctance of the Romans, when they were pressed to marriage by Augustus, sufficiently marks that the prevailing institutions were least favourable to the males. A specious theory is confuted by this free and perfect experiment, which demonstrates that the liberty of divorce does not contribute to happiness and virtue. The facility of separation would destroy all mutual confidence, and inflame every trifling dispute : the minute difference between a husband and a stranger, which might so easily be removed, might still more easily be forgotten ; and the matron who in five years can submit to the embraces of eight husbands, must cease to reverence the chastity of her own person."

Positivism, profiting by the lessons of the past, retains and perfects the institution of marriage as organised by Catholicism. It perfects that institution by introducing the conception of eternal widowhood. Re-marriage after the death of husband or wife is not absolutely forbidden ; it is within the scope of the civil power to allow it, but religion does not invest such marriage with its holy sanctions. The perpetual union of one man and one woman, as contemplated by Positivism, is an ideal type to which it is desirable that an approach should be made, but which can never be universally realised in practice. Marriage indissoluble even by death is the rule, the highest law of human existence: divorce, separation, and marriage as a mere life-contract, are to be regarded as exceptions to this rule, exceptions which are rendered necessary by man's weakness and by the disturbances which would ensue if that weakness were not to some extent indulged.*

The great point at issue between Comte and Mill, it appears to us, is this :—In organising society, are we simply to give full scope to the idiosyncracy of the individual, or are we to subordinate the individual to the community? With Mill the individual is all in all, with Comte the larger aggregate is of primary importance. With Mill each member of society is a separate and independent centre, with Comte, as with St. Paul, "we are every one members one of another."

I have the honor to be,

Sir,

Yours obediently,

A POSITIVIST.

October 10, 1868.

7.—REVD. DR. M. MITCHELL ON COMTE.

SIR,—In a lecture recently delivered, at Bombay, by the Revd. Dr. Murray Mitchell, on the subject of 'Young Bengal,' the following passage occurs : " Comtism, from causes that could be stated, but which I need not state here, has some influence (in Calcutta) ; and it is of course a most baneful influence."

---

* "The spirit of Positivism being always relative, concessions may be made to meet exceptional cases, without weakening or contradicting the principle ; whereas the absolute character of theological doctrine was incompatible with concession. The rules of morality should be general and comprehensive ; but in their practical applications exceptions have often to be made.   *   *   *   *   To the spirit of anarchy, however, Positivism yields nothing." *General View of Posi-tivism*. p. 254.

We beg to offer a few observations upon this concise but very decided anathema. *First* the term *Comtism* is not accepted by Positivists as one correctly indicating their peculiar point of view. There is, we admit, nothing disrespectful in the term, and it is no doubt employed, upon most occasions, quite innocently. Positivists, however, discard it because they do not regard their system as simply the outgrowth of a single mind. To regard it thus would be altogether inconsistent with the fundamental idea of Humanity upon which their religion is founded. Although Comte is certainly destined to occupy a very prominent place in the history of the world, still Positivism is not to be regarded as emanating solely from him. He placed the keystone upon the arch it is true, but the arch itself had been prepared for the crowning work of his master-hand by the patient labours of many previous generations. The whole world in fact has been labouring through all past time, unconsciously it may be but none the less surely, to give birth to a truly Catholic doctrine. Those who accept Positivism believe that it unfolds this doctrine, that it reveals to them at length the one increasing purpose that runs through all the ages. *Secondly,* when Dr. Mitchell asserts that Comtism has produced a most baneful influence upon certain minds in Bengal, does he mean to convey to his hearers only his own personal opinion in regard to the tendencies of a system which aims at organisation "irrespectively of God or king;" or does he make a deliberate statement resting upon a well-ascertained basis of fact? His brief but sweeping accusation leaves us quite in the dark as to the grounds upon which it was made. As Dr. Mitchell is one who exhorts and rebukes with authority, and as many of the views which he enunciates are readily welcomed by large classes in this country, it is by all means incumbent upon him, when passing judgment on the beliefs of other men, to weigh very carefully the substance and import of his words. Now Positivism is a subject which either should not have been mentioned at all in a popular discourse, or, if alluded to, should have been treated in such a way as to convey some definite and reliable information to those whom the lecturer was addressing. For ourselves, we were certainly surprised to learn, from Dr. Mitchell's remarks, that Comte's doctrines were understood, in this part of India, sufficiently well to have produced an appreciable influence of any kind. It would of course be an insult to the candour and learning of Dr. Mitchell to suppose that he would ascribe to the characteristic teaching of Positivism any results that followed only from a superficial acquaintance with the most elementary principles of the Positive Philosophy. In fact since Dr. Mitchell speaks of Comtism in connection with the religious state of educated men in Calcutta, it is evident that he includes in it something more than a simple adherence to certain scientific tenets. Assuming then that Dr. Mitchell refers to Positivism as a social and religious doctrine, we are somewhat curious to know if he has had any practical experience of its baneful influence upon the minds of individuals with whom he is well acquainted. If not he is scarcely justified in employing such language as that which we have quoted above, before an audience of which the greater part would probably know very little, or even nothing at all, concerning Comte, and would therefore be wholly dependent for information upon the *ipse dixit* of the lecturer. Our own experience, limited though it be would lead us to a conclusion very different from the one at which Dr. Mitchell has arrived; for we have known instances (though, every few we readily admit) in which Positivism, when rightly understood, has produced the most beneficial effects, by affording a wholesome corrective for the evils which arise from that negative condition of thought which is now so prevalent in all communities deeply penetrated by the spirit of Western Rationalism. We have never met with any instance in which a thorough knowledge of Positivism has been attended with injury, and we feel convinced that no earnest inquirer can peruse such works as the 'Catechism' and the 'Positive Politics' without being favorably influenced by the moral enthusiasm which pervades them, or, if his ancestral faith has already suffered shipwreck, without acquiring convictions which will render him both a wiser and a better man.

When Dr. Mitchell has again occasion to speak of Positivism in public we trust that he will support his unfavourable verdict with some solid proof. Until he does this we can attach no value whatever to his opinion. Mere random expressions of disapproval may mislead the ignorant and confirm the prejudiced, but are not calculated to find much favor with those who are impartial or thoroughly well-informed. The morality of criticism, be it remembered, has reached that stage of progress when men in general are no longer willing to tolerate misrepresentation and abuse in the place of argument. Competent knowledge and the exercise of strict justice are now demanded from all those who claim the privilege of acting as the instructors of their fellow-men.

I am, Sir,

Yours obediently,

A POSITIVIST.

January 8, 1870.

8.—PROPERTY AND ITS DUTIES.

SIR,—In the articles which have lately appeared in your columns on the subject of Perpetuities, an attempt has been made to consider the question from a social or moral point of view. It has apparently been assumed that a satisfactory decision can be arrived at by employing the narrow logic of the advocate in interpreting a few obscure texts which may, in fact, be made to mean anything. Surely it would have been the better plan, in such a case, to read the history of the past in a catholic spirit, with a view to profit by its real lessons and to draw from it principles which might serve as a guide in the exigencies of the future.

The critical discussion of sacred texts appears to be a favourite method nowadays for solving every social or political problem. The peculiarity of this method is that it may be applied so as to lead to any desired result. The grand old theocrats of India are often made to convict themselves, as it were, out of their own mouths, and are infallibly proved to have advocated doctrines and institutions which most probably they never could have conceived. or would have indignantly repudiated if they had been made acquainted with them. Thus, to take one instance out of several that might be adduced, it is the fashion at present to assume that perpetual widowhood is thoroughly pernicious, and then to support this assumption by showing that such a custom has no foundation in the Shastras—as if the unanimous consent and the time-honoured traditions of a great people were not sufficient sanctions in themselves, and at the same time sufficient evidence that the custom was firmly rooted in the religion of their ancestors. If the custom has really become a pernicious one, let the reformers of Hindustan attempt to abolish or modify it upon social grounds alone, and let them scorn to rest their case upon the interpretation of texts which were never intended to sustain the corroding criticism of innovators and unbelievers.

The question of Perpetuities is just one of those which seems to offer an admirable opportunity for the more advanced minds in Bengal to come forward and furnish their countrymen with a truly social doctrine. The records of the past, if taken as a whole and interpreted according to their general tenour, would surely indicate that ancient priests and legislators never regarded property, under any of its forms, as something which a man might dispose of solely according to his own caprice, which he might use or abuse as seemed to him best in his own sight. On the contrary the individual in ancient times was always bound to consult the interests of his community, his family, or his religion. The family-system as it obtains in India at the present day affords in itself ample evidence that the individual was never permitted to spend his wealth merely upon his own selfish and vicious gratifications during his lifetime, or to control its distribution exactly as he pleased after his death. It is only since the irrevocable decline of the old social and religious spirit that individuals have endeavoured to usurp an unlimited power over certain kinds of property. Owing to the absence of any organic doctrine this usurpation has been too largely tolerated, and as a natural consequence the grossest selfishness and most contemptuous disregard of the public good have prevailed throughout a large portion of the aristocratic and wealthy classes. But though society has permitted the individual, during his lifetime, to squander upon ignoble pleasures that stock of wealth which has been entrusted to his keeping, yet it has never fully acknowledged his absolute right to appropriate such wealth, after his death, to any purposes that might be dictated by his own lawless imagination. The attempt indeed has been made, notably by one Mr. Thelusson. This highly ingenious egoist made a will in which he directed the income of his property to be accumulated during the lives of all his childern, grand-children, and great-grand-children who were living at the time of his death, for the benefit of some future descendants to be living at the decease of the survivor. The State in this case justly intervened, and an act was passed to prevent the repetition of a practice which a learned English legist has aptly characterised as "a cruel absurdity."

As we believe that Positivism is the only doctrine which can furnish a satisfactory solution of the great social and moral problems which now claim the attention of statesmen and reformers both in the West and in the East, we propose in what follows to give an outline of the Positivist theory of property. Property, according to Positivism, is in its nature social and needs control. It does not, as sometimes represented, confer an absolute right upon the possessor, irrespectively of the good or bad use made of it. Property can neither be created nor even transferred by the sole agency of its possessor. The co-operation of the public is always necessary, whether in the assertion of the general principle or in the application of it to each special case. Therefore the tenure of property is not to be regarded as a purely individual right. In every age and in every country the state has intervened, to a greater or less degree, making property subservient to social requirements. Taxation evidently gives the public an interest in the fortune of each individual; an interest which instead of diminishing with the progress of civilisation has been always on the increase, especially in modern times, now that the connection of each member of society with the whole is becoming more apparent.

Positivism insists that wealth should be devoted to the continuous service of the community. It regards proprietorship as an important social function; the function, namely, of creating and administering that capital by means of which each generation lays the foundation for the operation of its successor.

Abandoning all useless and irritating discussion as to the origin of wealth and the extent of its possession, Positivism proceeds at once to the moral rules which should regulate it as a social function. The regulations required should be moral, not political in their source; general, not special, in their application. Those who accept them will do so of their own free will, under the influence of their education. By converting private property into a public function, Positivism would subject it to no tyrannical interference; for this, by the destruction of man's free impulse and responsibility, would prove most deeply degrading to man's character. The true principle of Positivism is, that all forces shall work together for the common good. With this view we have on the one hand to determine precisely what it is that the common good requires; and on the other, to develop the temper of mind most likely to satisfy the requirements. The conditions requisite for these two objects, are a recognised code of principles, an adequate education, and a healthy direction of public opinion.

Positivism adopts the institution of Inheritance. The mode of transmitting wealth is really that which is most likely to call out the temper requisite for its right employment. It saves the mind and the heart from the mean and sordid habits which are so often engendered by slow accumulation of capital. The man who is born to wealth is more likely to feel the wish to be respected. And thus those whom we are inclined to condemn as idlers may very easily become the most useful of the rich classes, under a wise re-organisation of opinions and habits. Of course too, since with the advance of civilisation the difficulty of living without industry increases, the class here referred to becomes more and more exceptional.

The preceding outline has been taken from Comte's General View of Positivism. To adapt the theory to the wants of India at the present time, considerable modifications would of course be required. It is not for us to point out these modifications. Our only object in bringing this theory forward is to present a noble ideal to all those who are interested in the welfare of their fellow-men, and to make it clear to them that no lasting good can be obtained by any measure of reform unless we have a definite social end in view. We regard the attempt to introduce Perpetuities into the customary law of the Hindoos, as thoroughly anti-social and as utterly at variance with the real spirit of Hindooism itself as disclosed to us in that complex but much abused organisation which will ever bear witness to the wonderful sagacity and rare persuasive powers of the early theocratic legislators. Those who are ambitious to follow in their steps and to emulate their well-earned glory, should reflect upon the noble self-abnegation which they manifested and upon the countless benefits which they undoubtedly secured to the community at large for many successive generations. If their work is now growing obsolete, let it not be forgotten that it has done good service in the past, and that the task of re-organisation should be accomplished in the same spirit of reverence and love which animated these good and faithful servants of Humanity.

I am, Sir,

Yours obediently,

May 7, 1870.   A POSITIVIST.